# The First World War

SIR MICHAEL HOWARD CBE is Emeritus
Professor of Modern History at both Oxford
and Yale Universities. His many books include
*The Causes of War*, *War in European History*,
*The Lessons of History*, *The Invention of Peace*,
*The Oxford History of the Twentieth Century*
(edited with W.R. Louis), *War and the Liberal
Conscience*, *The Franco-Prussian War* (Duff
Cooper Memorial Prize), and *Studies in War
and Peace* (Wolfson History Prize).

# The First World War

MICHAEL HOWARD

OXFORD
UNIVERSITY PRESS

# OXFORD

### UNIVERSITY PRESS

Great Clarendon Street, Oxford OX2 6DP

Oxford University Press is a department of the University of Oxford.
It furthers the University's objective of excellence in research, scholarship,
and education by publishing worldwide in

Oxford New York

Auckland Bangkok Buenos Aires Cape Town Chennai
Dar es Salaam Delhi Hong Kong Istanbul Karachi Kolkata
Kuala Lumpur Madrid Melbourne Mexico City Mumbai Nairobi
São Paulo Shanghai Singapore Taipei Tokyo Toronto

and an associated company in Berlin

Oxford is a registered trade mark of Oxford University Press
in the UK and in certain other countries

Published in the United States
by Oxford University Press Inc., New York

British Library Cataloguing in Publication Data

Data available

Library of Congress Cataloging in Publication Data

Data available

ISBN 0–19–285362–7

1 3 5 7 9 10 8 6 4 2

Typeset in New Baskerville
by RefineCatch Limited, Bungay, Suffolk
Printed in Great Britain
on acid-free paper by
Biddles Ltd., Guildford and King's Lynn

# Foreword

This book, as its title suggests, is intended simply to introduce the vast subject of the First World War to those who know little or nothing about it.

Anyone who ventures more deeply into the subject will find that behind almost every sentence in the book lies a scholarly controversy that still remains unsettled, and that what looks like a simple and uncontroversial narrative will appear to some as highly biased and selective. Certainly not everyone will agree with the view that it was the ruling circles in Imperial Germany who were ultimately responsible, both for the outbreak and for the continuance of the war. But an account of the war that would satisfy everyone, even if it were possible, could certainly not be written in the space available, and even if it could it would be almost unreadable.

There may be those who complain that too much attention is devoted to the military, and not enough to the social, economic, or psychological dimensions of the subject. For this I make no apology. These non-military factors are vital for understanding why the war took place at all. But once the war began events on the battlefield ultimately determined what happened on the home front, and were responsible for the vast transformation that resulted in the entire structure of European society.

My thanks are due to George Miller who made me write

the book in the first place, to Hilary Walford and Rebecca O'Connor who converted my typescript into a publishable text, and to Dr Gary Sheffield who expertly steered me through the endless controversies about the conduct of operations on the Western Front.

Michael Howard

# Contents

# List of Illustrations

While every effort has been made to secure permissions, we
may have failed in a few cases to trace the copyright holder.
We apologize for any apparent negligence.

# Maps

1 Europe before the war

2  Europe after the war

Railway ........
Front line 1915–16 ▬▬▬

3 The Western Front

4 The Eastern Front

5 The Balkans

6  Northern Italy

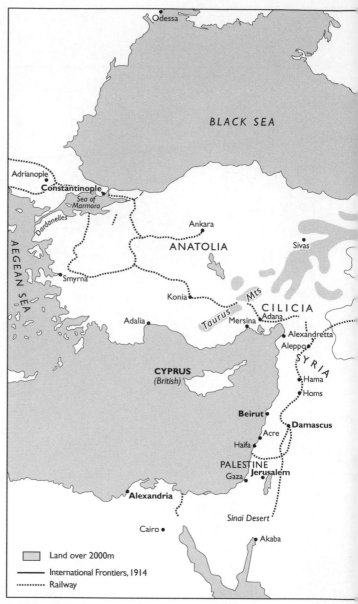

7 The Ottoman Empire

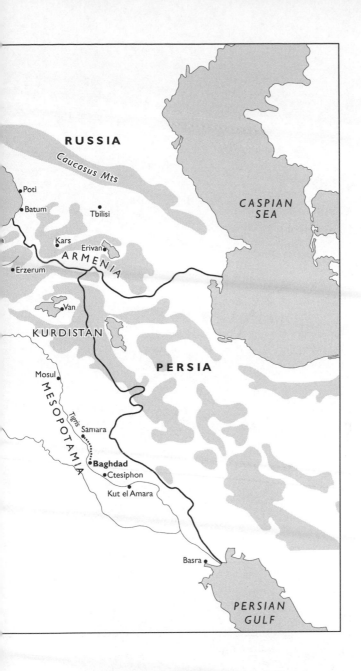

# Europe in 1914

S ince the Great War of 1914–18 was fought on all the oceans of the world and ultimately involved belligerents from every continent, it can justifiably be termed a 'world war'. But it was certainly not the first. European powers had been fighting each other all over the globe for the previous 300 years. Those who fought in it called it simply 'the Great War'. Like all its predecessors, it began as a purely European conflict, arising out of the conflicting ambitions and mutual fears of the European powers. That its course should have been so terrible, and its consequences so catastrophic, was the result not so much of its global scale as of a combination of military technology and the culture of the peoples who fought it. Karl von Clausewitz had written in the aftermath of the Napoleonic Wars that war was a trinity composed of the policy of the government, the activities of the military, and 'the passions of the peoples'. Each of these must be taken into account if we are to understand both why the war happened and why it took the course that it did.

## *The European Powers in 1914*

With a few marginal changes, the 'Great Powers' of Europe (as they were still called) were much the same as they had been for the previous two centuries, but the balance between them had changed radically. The most powerful of all was now the German Empire, created by the Kingdom of Prussia as a result of its victorious wars of 1866 against the Austrian Empire and 1870 against France. France had been reduced by her defeat to second-rank status and resented it. The polyglot lands of the Austrian Empire had been reorganized since 1867 as the Dual Monarchy of Austria-Hungary, and accepted subordinate status as an ally of Germany. Although Hungary was a quasi-autonomous state, the Monarchy was often referred to simply as 'Austria' and its peoples as 'Austrians', much as the United Kingdom was commonly known abroad as 'England' and its people 'English'. Flanking these continental powers were two empires only partially European in their interests: the huge semi-Asiatic Russian Empire, a major if intermittent player in south-east Europe; and Britain, whose main concern was to maintain a balance of power on the Continent while she expanded and consolidated her possessions overseas. Spain, the last vestiges of whose overseas empire (apart from a coastal fringe of North Africa) had been lost to the United States at the beginning of the century, had dwindled to third rank. Her place in the cast had been taken by an Italy whose unification under the House of Savoy between 1860 and 1871 had been more apparent than real, but whose nuisance value alone won her the wary respect of the other powers.

Until the end of the eighteenth century, these powers had

been socially homogeneous. All were still primarily agrarian societies dominated by a landed aristocracy and ruled by historic dynasties legitimized by an established Church. A hundred years later all this had either been completely transformed or was in the course of rapid and destabilizing transformation; but the pace of change had been very uneven, as we shall see.

## *Britain*

Britain had led the way. By the beginning of the twentieth century she was already a fully urbanized and industrialized nation. The landed aristocracy remained socially dominant, but the last vestiges of political power were being wrested from it by a House of Commons in which the two major parties competed for the votes, not just of the middle, but increasingly, as the franchise was extended, of the working classes. A liberal–radical coalition came to power in 1906 and began to lay the foundations of a welfare state, but it could not ignore the paradoxical predicament in which Britain found herself at the beginning of the century. She was still the wealthiest power in the world and the proud owner of the greatest empire that the world had ever seen; but she was more vulnerable than ever before in her history. At the hub of that empire was a densely populated island dependent on world trade for its wealth and, yet more important, for imported foodstuffs to feed its cities. The Royal Navy's 'command of the seas' both held the Empire together and ensured that the British people were fed. Loss of naval supremacy was a nightmare that dogged successive British governments and dominated their relations with other powers. Ideally they would have wished to remain aloof from European disputes, but any indication that their neighbours were showing signs, singly or collectively, of threatening their naval dominance had for the previous twenty years been a matter of anguished national concern.

### France

For over a century, between 1689 and 1815, Britain's major rival for world power had been France, and it had taken nearly another 100 years for her to realize that this was no longer the case. France had lagged far behind in the economic development that could have made her a serious competitor. The Revolution of 1789 had destroyed the three pillars of the *Ancien Régime*—monarchy, noblesse, and Church—and distributed their lands among peasant smallholders who remained staunchly resistant to any development, whether reaction or further revolution, that threatened to expropriate them; and their pattern of life did not encourage either the growth of population or the accumulation of capital that made economic development possible. In 1801 the population of France had totalled twenty-seven million and was the largest in Europe. In 1910 it was still only thirty-five million, whereas over the same period that of Britain had risen from eleven million to forty million, while that of the newly united Germany was over sixty-five million and still rising. After its demoralizing defeat in 1870, the French army had found an outlet in African conquests that created friction with Britain's imperial interests, as did traditional rivalries in the eastern Mediterranean, but for the French people these were marginal issues. They remained deeply divided between those who had profited from the Revolution; those who, under the leadership of the Catholic Church, still refused to come to terms with it; and an increasingly powerful socialist movement that wanted to push it a stage further. France remained both wealthy and culturally dominant, but her domestic politics were highly volatile. Abroad, the German annexation of Alsace and Lorraine in 1871 had been neither forgotten nor forgiven, and fear of German power made France anxiously dependent upon her only major ally—Russia.

## Russia

The other continental rival feared by Britain in the nineteenth century was the huge Russian Empire, whose expansion to the south and east threatened both the route to India through the Middle East (which had led Britain to prop up the moribund Turkish Empire) and the frontiers of India itself. Certainly Russia's potential was (as it remains) enormous, but it was limited (as it still is) by the backwardness of its society and the inefficiency of its government.

Capitalism and industrialization came late to Russia, and then largely as a result of foreign investment and expertise. At the beginning of the twentieth century the Czars ruled over a population of 164 million, consisting overwhelmingly of peasants who had been emancipated from actual serfdom only a generation earlier. They still exercised an absolutism such as Western Europe had never known—supported by an

Orthodox Church untouched by any Reformation, and through the instrumentality of a vast and lethargic bureaucracy. The educated elites were divided between 'Westerners', who, looking to Europe as a model, were attempting to introduce economic development and responsible government, and 'Slavophiles', who considered such ideas degenerate and wished to preserve historic Slav culture. But successive military defeats—at the hands of the French and British in 1855–6 and the Japanese in 1904–5—drove home the lesson learned by Peter the Great, that military power abroad depended on both political and economic development at home. Serfdom had been abolished after the Crimean War, and representative institutions of a kind introduced after defeat and near-revolution in 1905. Railway development had enormously boosted industrial production in the 1890s, bringing Russia, in the view of some economists, to the point of economic 'take-off'. But the regime remained terrified that industrial development, however essential it might be for military effectiveness, would only encourage demands for further political reform, and it suppressed dissidents with a brutality that only drove them to extremes of 'terrorism' (a term and technique invented by Russian revolutionaries in the nineteenth century), thus justifying further brutality. This made her an embarrassing, even if a necessary, ally for the liberal West.

At the end of the nineteenth century the attention of the Russian government had been focused on expansion into Asia, but after its defeat by the Japanese in 1904–5 it was switched to south-east Europe, which was still dominated by the Ottoman Empire. There national resistance movements, originally based on the Orthodox Christian communities in

Greece, Serbia, and Bulgaria, had traditionally looked to the Russians for sponsorship—first as fellow-Christians, then as fellow-Slavs. All three had established independent states in the course of the nineteenth century. But there were also large numbers of Slavs, especially of Serbs and their cousins the Croats, in Austria-Hungary; and, the more successful the new Slav nations were in establishing their identity and independence, the more apprehensive the Habsburgs became about the increasing restiveness of their own minorities, and the part played by Russia in encouraging it.

## *Austria-Hungary*

In Western Europe—Britain, France, Germany, Italy, even Russia—nationalism was a cohesive force, though such 'submerged nations' as the Poles and the Irish were already struggling for independence. But the Habsburg Monarchy consisted entirely of 'submerged nations'. In the eighteenth century there had been a dominant German elite, but even for the Germans there was now an adjacent homeland in the new German Empire to the north. In 1867 the Habsburg Empire had transformed itself into the 'Dual Monarchy' by granting the most powerful submerged nation, the Magyars, quasi-independence in the Kingdom of Hungary, which shared with the dominantly German 'Austrians' only a monarch (the Emperor Franz-Joseph, who had ruled since 1848), an army, a treasury, and a foreign office. The Magyars, like the Germans (and indeed the British, whom they greatly admired and whose parliament building they imitated in

Budapest), considered themselves a master race, and they ruled oppressively over their own Slav minorities—Slovaks, Rumanians, and Croats. In the western half of the Monarchy the German 'Austrians' ruled not only Slavs to the north (Czechs), north-east (Poles and Ruthenes), and south (Slovenes and Serbs), but Italian-speaking lands on the southern slopes of the Alps coveted by the new Kingdom of Italy. Unlike the tough Magyar squireens of Budapest, the rational bureaucrats of Vienna tried to treat their subject-nationalities tolerantly and granted them equal rights with the Germans. The result was to paralyse the machinery of government in Vienna and force the Emperor to rule by decree. Its rich mixture of cultures certainly made Vienna a city with a uniquely vibrant intellectual and artistic life, but its intelligentsia looked to the future with apprehension and occasionally despair.

### Germany

Finally there was Imperial Germany, the most complex and problematic power of them all.

The unification of Germany in 1871 had created a nation that combined the most dynamic economy in Europe with a regime that in many respects had hardly emerged from feudalism. The Hohenzollern dynasty had ruled Prussia through a bureaucracy and an army that were both drawn from a 'service gentry' (*Junkers*) rooted primarily in their eastern provinces. They resented the very existence of a *Reichstag* (parliament) that had been unsuccessfully aspiring to power ever since the middle of the nineteenth century. In the newly united empire the *Reichstag* represented the whole range of the enlarged German population: agrarian conservatives with their vast estates in the east, industrialists in the north and west, Bavarian Roman Catholic farmers in the south, and, increasingly as the economy developed, the industrial working classes, with their socialist leaders, in the valleys of the Rhine and the Ruhr. The *Reichstag* voted the budget, but the government was appointed by, and was responsible to, the monarch, the Kaiser. The chief intermediary between *Reichstag* and Kaiser was the Chancellor. The first holder of that office, Otto von Bismarck, had used the authority he derived from the Kaiser to make the *Reichstag* do his own bidding. His successors were little more than messengers informing the *Reichstag* of the Kaiser's decisions and manipulating them to ensure the passage of the budget. By the Kaiser himself they were seen almost as household servants, of considerably less importance than the Chief of the General Staff.

Under these circumstances the personality of the Kaiser was of overwhelming importance, and it was the misfortune not only of Germany but of the entire world that at this juncture the House of Hohenzollern should have produced, in Wilhelm II, an individual who in his person embodied three qualities that can be said to have characterized the contemporary German ruling elite: archaic militarism, vaulting ambition, and neurotic insecurity.

Militarism was institutionalized in the dominant role that the army had played in the culture of the old Prussia it had dominated and had to a large extent created; much as its victories over Austria and France had created the new

1 Kaiser Wilhelm II: the incarnation of 'Prussian militarism'

German Empire. In the new Germany the army was socially dominant, as it had been in the old Prussia—a dominance spread throughout all classes by three-year universal military service. The bourgeoisie won the cherished right to wear uniform by taking up commissions in the reserve, and imitated the habits of the *Junker* military elite. At a lower level, retired NCOs dominated their local communities. The Kaiser appeared always in uniform as the All Highest War Lord, surrounded by a military entourage. Abroad, this militarism, with its constant parades and uniforms and celebrations of the victories of 1870, was seen as absurd rather than sinister; and so it might have been if it had not been linked with the second quality—ambition.

Bismarck himself, having created the German Empire, had been content simply to preserve it, but the successor generation was not so easily satisfied. It had every reason to be ambitious. It constituted a nation over sixty million strong with a superb heritage of music, poetry, and philosophy, and whose scientists, technologists, and scholars (not to mention soldiers) were the envy of the world. Its industrialists had already surpassed the British in the production of coal and steel, and together with the scientists were pioneering a new 'industrial revolution' based on chemicals and electricity. The Germans prided themselves on a uniquely superior culture that held the balance between the despotic barbarism of their eastern neighbours and the decadent democracy of the West. But within this proud, prosperous, and successful nation a deep cleavage was developing, which only grew deeper as its prosperity increased. The growth of its industries increased the size and influence of a working class whose leaders, while no longer revolutionary, were increasingly pressing for an extension of democracy and the abolition of social privilege, and whose party, the Social Democrats, had become by 1914 the largest in the *Reichstag*.

The possessing classes had their own quarrels, mainly between the landowners of the east and the industrialists of the west, but they made common cause against what they saw as a socialist revolutionary threat. From the beginning of the twentieth century they began to combat it by a 'forward policy' based on the assertion of 'national greatness'. With the Kaiser at their head, German right-wing political leaders began to claim for Germany the status, not only of a Great Power, but of a World Power, *Weltmacht*. The only competitor in that class was the British Empire; but if she was to compete with Britain, Germany needed, not only a great army, but a great fleet. To raise money for such a fleet a major propaganda exercise was necessary; and that propaganda could be effective only if Britain was depicted as the next great adversary that the Germans must overcome if they were to achieve the status that they believed to be rightfully their due.

### The Rival Alliances

Germany already saw herself surrounded by enemies. When Bismarck created the German Empire in 1871, he knew very well that the natural reaction of her neighbours would be to unite against her, and he took care to see that this did not happen. France, with good reason, he regarded as irreconcilable, if only because she had been compelled to surrender her provinces of Alsace and Lorraine. He therefore tried to neutralize her by encouraging the colonial ambitions that would bring her into conflict with Britain, and ensured that she could find no allies among the other powers of Europe by binding them all into his own system of alliances. The Dual Monarchy presented no difficulty. Beset with internal problems, she had been happy to conclude the Dual Alliance with Germany in 1879. Her own natural enemy was the newly unified Italy, who coveted the Italian-speaking lands on the southern slopes of the Alps and at the head of the Adriatic that still remained in Austrian hands; but Bismarck linked both into a Triple Alliance by supporting Italian territorial claims against France and her Mediterranean possessions.

There remained the two flanking powers, Russia and Britain. Russia would be a formidable ally for the French if given the chance, which Bismarck was determined that she should not have. He had been careful to cultivate her friendship and had linked her into his 'system' by an alliance concluded in 1881 and renewed, as a 'Reinsurance Treaty', six years later. As for Britain, France and Russia were her natural adversaries, so to have them held in check by a strong central power suited British statesmen very well. The one thing that Bismarck had good reason to fear was a war in the Balkans between Austria and Russia that might upset the balance that he had so precariously established. At the Congress of Berlin in 1878 he brokered an agreement that divided the Balkans into spheres of influence between Russia and the Dual Monarchy, and gave to the latter a 'Protectorate' over the most northerly and turbulent of the Ottoman provinces, Bosnia-Herzegovina. This settlement produced an uneasy peace that lasted until the end of the century, but Bismarck's 'system' had begun to unravel long before then.

Bismarck's successors, for a whole complex of reasons, failed to renew the treaty with Russia, thus leaving her available as an ally for France. It was a terrible mistake. For Russia, if this newly powerful Germany was not an ally, she was a threat, and one that could be countered only by a military alliance with France. France was in any case a plentiful source of the investment capital that Russia needed to finance the modernization of her economy. So in 1891 the two powers concluded a treaty, the Dual Entente, to confront the Triple Alliance, and the rival groups began to compete in the enhancement of their military power.

The British initially regarded this alliance between her traditional adversaries with alarm, and the dynamics of international relations would normally have dictated an alliance with Germany as a natural consequence. That this did not happen was due partly to the traditional British reluctance to become involved in any entangling continental alliances, and partly to extraordinarily clumsy German diplomacy. More important than either, however, was the German decision that we have already noted, to build a navy that could challenge the British command of the seas.

Given that she already had the most powerful army in the world, it was not immediately evident—at least not to the British—why Germany needed an ocean-going navy at all. Hitherto, in spite of industrial competition, British relations with Germany had been friendly rather than otherwise. But now there began a 'naval race', for quantitative and qualitative superiority in ships, that was to transform British public opinion. By 1914 Britain had pulled decisively ahead, if only because she was prepared to devote greater resources to shipbuilding and did not need, as did the Germans, to sustain the burden of an arms race by land as well. But the British remained concerned not so much with the fleet that Germany had already built as with that which she yet might—especially if a successful war gave her military hegemony over the Continent.

So Britain mended her fences with her traditional rivals. In 1904 she settled her differences with France in Africa, establishing a relationship that became known as *l'entente cordiale*. There remained the Russian Empire, whose southward expansion towards the frontiers of India had given Victorian statesmen continual nightmares, and had led the British in 1902 to conclude their first formal alliance for a nearly a century with the emerging power of Japan. Three years later Russia was defeated and brought to the verge of revolution by war with Japan, so in 1907 she was happy to conclude an agreement with Britain over the disputed borderlands of Persia and Afghanistan, thus creating a 'Triple Entente'. Beyond Europe, Britain took care to remain on friendly terms with the United States. American appetite for naval expansion had been whetted by victory over Spain in 1899 and annexation of her possessions in the Pacific, but British statesmen realized that America's immense resources meant that confrontation with her should be avoided at almost any cost. So traditional rivalries were appeased by the virtual abandonment of a British naval presence in the western hemisphere and the careful cultivation of a harmony between British and American elites based on 'Anglo-Saxon' consanguinity and shared political values.

Although Britain concluded no formal alliances except that with Japan, the Germans complained that the British were weaving a web to encircle and imprison them, and relations grew steadily worse. In 1911, when the Germans attempted to humiliate the French by challenging their influence in Morocco with a naval demonstration off Agadir, the British made their support for the French explicit. Many people in Britain and Germany began to regard each other as natural enemies, and war between them as inevitable.

But, when war did break out three years later, it was at the other end of Europe, in the Balkans, as Bismarck himself had gloomily foreseen.

## The Balkan Crises

Without Bismarck's calming hand, relations between Austria-Hungary and Russia had deteriorated as badly as those between Britain and Germany. The Balkan state that the Austrians most feared was Serbia, especially since their protectorate over Bosnia-Herzegovina had placed many Serbs under Austrian control. In 1903 a *coup d'état* in Belgrade had overthrown the Obrenovic dynasty that had pursued a course of conciliation towards the Dual Monarchy, and replaced it with a regime dedicated to the expansion of Serbia through the liberation of Serbs under foreign rule—especially those in Bosnia. Five years later Austria formally annexed Bosnia-Herzegovina to facilitate her control over those provinces. The Serb government responded by creating an open 'liberation movement' for Bosnian Serbs with a covert terrorist wing, 'the Black Hand', trained and supported by elements within the Serb army. At the same time, Serbia, with Russian encouragement, took the lead in forming a 'Balkan League' with Greece, Bulgaria, and

Montenegro, dedicated to the final expulsion of the Turks from the peninsula. Their opportunity came in 1912, when the Turks were engaged in defending their territories in Libya against an attack by Italy, whose government had grandiose ambitions (anticipating those of Mussolini a generation later) to restore the glories of the Roman Empire. In the First Balkan War of that year the Balkan allies drove the Turks from the entire peninsula except a bridgehead round Adrianople. A second war was fought the following year between the victorious allies over the division of the spoils.

As a result of these two wars, the territory and population of Serbia were doubled and her ambitions hugely encouraged. But in Vienna the reigning emotions were fear and frustration: fear at the apparently unstoppable march of Serbia, with all the encouragement this gave to Slav dissidents in both halves of the Monarchy; and frustration at their inability to do anything about it. Then on 28 July 1914 the heir to the Habsburg throne, Archduke Franz Ferdinand, was assassinated in Sarajevo, the capital of Bosnia-Herzegovina, by Gavril Princip, a teenage terrorist trained and armed by the Serb-sponsored Black Hand.

## 2

# The Coming of War

### *The Crisis of 1914*

The crisis precipitated by the Archduke's assassination at first seemed no worse than the half-dozen or so that had preceded it in the Balkans since 1908 and been peacefully resolved by the intervention of the Great Powers. But the Austrians were now determined to crush their Serbian enemy for good. They issued an ultimatum that would, if accepted, have turned Serbia virtually into a client state of the Dual Monarchy. This the Russians could not have tolerated, and the Austrians knew it; so before issuing their ultimatum they obtained what became known as 'a blank cheque' from Berlin, assuring them of German support in the event of war. In issuing that cheque the German government knew that it was risking at least a European war, but by now such a war was regarded in Berlin as almost inevitable. Germany's military leaders calculated that it would be better to have it sooner, while the Russians had still not fully recovered from the defeat of 1905, rather than three years later, when they would have completed a huge French-financed railway-building and mobilization programme that could put them in an entirely new league of military strength. France herself had been going through a phase of militant nationalism after the Agadir crisis, and was both militarily and psychologically ready for war. In Russia, Pan-Slav public opinion pressed strongly for war, even though the government knew very well the weakness not only of the army but of the entire regime, already shaken in 1905 by a revolution whose rumblings had not yet died away. As for the British, their interest in the affairs of the Balkans was minimal and their own domestic problems overwhelming; but if there was to be a European war, they were unlikely to stand by and watch France defeated by a Germany, many of whose publicists had for long been designating England as their principal enemy and for whom victory in Europe would be only the preliminary to her establishment as not just a Great, but a World Power.

Europe thus stood on the brink of war in July 1914. To understand why she toppled over we must now look at the other two elements in the Clausewitzian trinity: the activities of the military and the passions of the peoples. *caused*

### The Military Situation in 1914

The German victories of 1866–70 had opened a new chapter in the military as well as the political history of Europe. The German triumphs were generally seen to have been due to two factors, one strategic and one tactical. The first had been Germany's capacity to deploy very much larger forces in the field than could her adversaries, and this was itself due to two causes. One was the development of railways and telegraphs, which made possible the rapid deployment to the theatre of war of unprecedented numbers of men. The other was the introduction of universal peacetime conscription, which ensured not only that these numbers were available but that they had been fully trained and could be rapidly mobilized when required. Such armies—and by 1871 that of the Germans already numbered over a million—required an unprecedented degree of organization, which was the task of a general staff whose head became the effective commander-in-chief of the entire force. It also called for a devolution of command that imposed new responsibilities on middle-ranking and junior officers. Battles could no longer be fought and decided under the eye of a single commanding general. They might extend, as they did in the Russo-Japanese War, over many scores of miles. Once he had deployed his forces on the battlefield, the commander-in-chief could only sit in his headquarters many miles behind the front line and hope for the best.

This extension of the front was increased by the second factor, the development of long-range weapons. The introduction of breech-loading and rifled firearms for infantry increased both range and accuracy to an extent that would have made frontal attacks out of the question if simultaneous developments in artillery had not provided the firepower to support them. Even since 1870 ranges had increased enormously. By 1900 all European armies were equipped with infantry rifles sighted up to 1,000 yards and lethally accurate at half that range. Field guns were now ranged up to five miles, and capable of firing up to twenty rounds a minute. Heavy artillery, hitherto used only for siege work, was being rendered mobile by rail and road, and could engage targets at a range of over twenty-five miles. Armies would thus come under fire long before they could even see their enemy, let alone attack his positions.

In a pioneer work of operational analysis, *La Guerre future*, published in 1899, the Polish writer Ivan Bloch calculated that in wars fought with such weapons the offensive would in future be impossible. Battles would quickly degenerate into bloody deadlock. The cost of maintaining such huge armies in the field would be prohibitive. The economies of the belligerent powers would be overstrained, and the consequent hardships imposed on the civilian population would everywhere lead to the revolutions that the possessing classes throughout Europe were beginning to dread. So accurately did this foretell the course and outcome of the First World War that subsequent historians have wondered why more account of it was not taken at the time. But within a few years of its publication two wars were fought that showed that, although the new weapons certainly inflicted terrible losses, decisive battles could still be fought and won. In South Africa in 1899–1902, in spite of the skill and courage of the Boer riflemen, the British eventually won the war and pacified the country—very largely through the use of cavalry whose demise military reformers had been foreseeing for many years. More significantly, in 1904–5, in a war fought on both sides with the latest modern weapons, the Japanese had been able, by a combination of skilful infantry and artillery tactics and the suicidal courage of their troops, to defeat the Russians in battle after battle and compel them to sue for peace. The lesson learned by European armies was that victory was still possible for armies equipped with up-to-date weapons and whose soldiers were not afraid to die. But a further lesson was that the victory had to be quick. A campaign lasting little more than a year had resulted in revolution in Russia and brought Japan to the brink of economic collapse. Bloch's forecast that no nation could for long sustain a war fought, in the words of the German Chief of Staff Alfred von Schlieffen, by 'armies of millions of men costing milliards of marks', was taken to heart. The powers of Europe all prepared to fight a short war because they could not realistically contemplate fighting a long one; and the only way to keep the war short was by taking the offensive.

## The 'Arms Race'

In the first decade of the twentieth century the powers of Europe were engaged in a process of competitive modernization of their armed forces that came to be called, rather inaccurately, an 'arms race'. The lessons of the Russo-Japanese War were closely studied, especially by the Germans, who perceived long before their competitors the importance of entrenchments to protect their infantry from artillery fire, and the huge advantage given by mobile heavy artillery. Machine guns had also proved their value, but their rate of fire of 600 rounds per minute presented problems of ammunition supply that made their employment in mobile warfare highly problematic. All armies added them to their arsenals, but it was only in the defensive battles on the Western Front in 1915–17 that they came into their own. All armies abandoned their colourful uniforms (the British, accustomed to fighting in the dust and desert of colonial campaigns, had done so already) and clothed themselves in various shades of the mud in which they would now have to fight—except the French, who were compelled to retain their distinctive scarlet trousers by nostalgic nationalist politicians, and suffered terribly in consequence. All competed in introducing the new technology of the aeroplane and the automobile, although in 1914 the first was only just coming into use to supplement cavalry reconnaissance, and the second was used mainly for the transportation of staff officers and senior commanders. Throughout the war, transportation and traction beyond railheads were to remain overwhelmingly horse drawn. Once they left their trains, armies could still move no faster than those of Napoleon—indeed, of Julius Caesar. Finally, the importance of wireless communications—and their interception—was generally recognized, especially in naval warfare. But on land sets were still too heavy for operational use below army headquarters, with results for front-line fighting that we shall consider in due course.

In armament all European armies in 1914 were at least comparable. Only in their use of mobile heavy artillery were the Germans able to spring unpleasant surprises. What gave military planners sleepless nights was not the equipment of the enemy armed forces, but their size. This was ultimately determined by the size of the population, but it was also affected by social constraints that limited the extent and duration of conscription, and financial pressures limiting its cost. Of the three powers principally concerned, the population of the newly united German Empire at sixty-seven million exceeded, as we have seen, that of France at thirty-six million, but was far inferior to the 164 million of the Russian Empire. In France, democratic mistrust of militarism had confined military service to two years, but over 80 per cent of available manpower was called up. In Germany military service lasted for three years, but the numbers called up were constrained by both budgetary considerations and resistance from an increasingly left-wing *Reichstag*, as well as by reluctance within the army itself to recruiting within the growing and (it was thought) politically unreliable urban population. Only some 54 per cent of the manpower available was called up before 1911, which in 1911 gave the German army a peacetime strength of 612,000 as against the French of 593,000. The size of Russia's population and in consequence of her army (1,345,000) looked terrifying on paper, but it was made less impressive by shortage of railways to deploy it and the administrative incompetence so humiliatingly revealed by the defeat in 1905. So negligible had the Russian threat then appeared that Schlieffen, in the 'plan' he bequeathed in that year to his successor, virtually ignored it altogether and concentrated the entire strength of the German army against France.

The Russian defeat in 1905 may have reassured the Germans, but it terrified the French. After 1908 they began to pour money into Russia to build up her economic infrastructure (in particular her railways) and re-equip her armies in a 'Great Programme' of military reform that was due for completion in 1917. It was now the Germans' turn to be alarmed. They could no longer underrate the importance of Austria-Hungary as an ally, and there was much wild talk in both countries about the Slav threat to Western civilization. The constraints on the Germans' own military build-up disappeared, and in 1912 they introduced a crash programme of expansion that increased the size of their army by 1914 to

864,000. The French responded by increasing their own length of military service to three years, giving them a peacetime strength of 700,000. In both countries the additional expenditure was rushed through parliaments increasingly convinced of the imminence of a war in which their national existence would be at stake. When war did break out in 1914 the Germans and French each mobilized about four million men, of which some 1.7 million Germans and two million French confronted each other on the Western Front.

### The Decision for War

Such was the situation when the Austrians delivered their ultimatum to Serbia in July 1914. The Austrians were determined to crush the Serbs, if necessary by using military force, and relied on their German ally to hold the Russians in check while they did so. The Germans were confident that they could deter Russia from intervening, but even if they did not, they preferred to go to war while their army was at the peak of its strength, rather than delay while the balance of military power tipped inexorably in favour of their adversaries. The one thing they did not contemplate was letting the Austrians down. The Dual Monarchy was their only remaining ally (quite rightly they discounted the Italians), and its humiliation and likely disintegration would be catastrophic for German prestige and power. But very similar calculations were being made in Russia. For the Russians, to abandon Serbia would be to betray the whole Slav cause and lose everything that had been gained in the Balkans since the beginning of the century. Finally, for the French, to abandon

Russia to defeat would be peacefully to acquiesce in a German hegemony of Europe and her own reduction to the rank of a third-rate power.

All this was quite clear in Berlin. By supporting the Austrians the Germans knew that they were risking a European war, but one that they expected to win. The only question was, would it also be a world war? Would Britain be brought in as well?

This was a possibility whose implications had been barely considered in Berlin, where decision-makers were in a state of what psychologists have termed 'cognitive dissonance'. Britain was widely seen as Germany's ultimate enemy, the adversary who must be faced down if Germany were to attain her rightful status as a World Power. Yet Britain had been virtually ignored in German military planning. The army had left it to the navy, assuming that any expeditionary force Britain sent to help the French would be too small to worry about. But the German navy could do nothing—or believed it could do nothing—until it built up a high seas fleet capable of challenging the Royal Navy, which it was not yet in a position to do. For Germany's Minister for the Navy, Admiral Graf von Tirpitz, the timing of the war was disastrous. Any British expeditionary force on the Continent might be caught up in the defeat of its allies, but that had happened before (as it was to happen again) in European history; but the war could still have gone on as it had in the days of Napoleon—a prolonged war of the kind for which no one had planned and which it was generally believed that no one could win.

The German government was thus gambling on British neutrality, and in July 1914 this seemed a reasonable bet.

Since 1906 the hands of the British government had been full with industrial unrest at home and an apparently imminent civil war in Ireland. Ever since the Agadir crisis in 1911 British military leaders had been holding informal but detailed staff discussions with their French colleagues about the possible dispatch of an expeditionary force to the Continent, but the government had not thought it wise to reveal these to a largely pacifistic parliament. The Royal Navy had made all its dispositions on the assumption of a war with Germany, but was committed to nothing. There was widespread concern at the thrust of German policy, but left-wing and liberal opinion remained solidly neutralist. Dislike of German 'militarism' was balanced by hostility to a despotic Russian regime whose pogroms against Jews and brutal persecution of dissidents were equally offensive to the liberal conscience. It was still widely believed that British imperial interests were threatened more by France and Russia than by Germany. Commercial and financial links with Germany remained close. Public opinion and parliamentary support thus remained too uncertain for the Foreign Secretary, Sir Edward Grey, to be able to give any unequivocal assurance that, if the crisis developed into war, Britain would take her place alongside her associates of the Triple Entente. Had Germany not invaded Belgium, it is an open question whether Britain would have maintained her neutrality and for how long. But invade her she did, and we must see why.

German military planners had faced one basic strategic problem since the days of Frederick the Great. Squeezed between a hostile France in the west and a hostile Russia in the east (usually joined by a hostile Austria in the south), their only hope of avoiding defeat had always been to overwhelm one of their enemies before the other was in a position to intervene. Prussian victories in 1866 and 1870 had been made possible by Bismarck's success in neutralizing Russia in both conflicts, but in 1891 the Franco-Russian Alliance had revived the dilemma in its starkest form. Which enemy should be destroyed first? Schlieffen had firmly settled for France. No decisive victory was possible in the huge plains of Poland, but, if France could be defeated, the Russians might quickly be brought to terms. But how to gain a rapid and decisive victory over France? Since 1871 France had built such formidable fortifications along her German frontier that a repeat of 1870 appeared impossible. The only answer seemed to lie in an outflanking movement through neutral Belgium, one powerful enough to defeat the French army in time to switch forces eastwards to ward off the expected Russian assault. Schlieffen himself, as we have seen, did not take the Russian threat very seriously, but by 1914 it appeared such a menace that German planners sometimes feared that Russian armies might enter Berlin before their own forces had reached Paris. A massive invasion through Belgium was thus an essential part of German war plans, and the increase in the size of the German army resulting from the reforms of 1912–13 had been largely devised to make this possible.

Clausewitz once wrote that military plans might have their own grammar but they had no inherent logic. There was certainly no logic in the decision by the German General Staff that, in order to support the Austrians in a conflict with Russia over Serbia, Germany should attack France, who was not party to the quarrel, and do so by invading Belgium, whose neutral status had been guaranteed by a treaty of 1831 to which both Germany and Britain had been signatories. It was significant of the state of affairs in Berlin that the German Chancellor, Theodore von Bethmann Hollweg, saw it as his task, not to query this decision, but to justify it as a necessary breach of international law in the prosecution of a just and defensive war. But, in order for the war to appear just and defensive, Russia must be made to appear the aggressor, and this was the major concern of the German government in the last days of the crisis.

Serbia predictably rejected the Austrian ultimatum, and Austria declared war on 28 July. Thereafter military calculations dominated decision making in every European capital. On 30 July Czar Nicholas II, with extreme hesitation, ordered the mobilization of all Russian armed forces. It was generally assumed that mobilization led inevitably to *Aufmarsch*, the deployment of armies for the invasion of their neighbours, and that such deployment led with equal inevitability to war. Mobilization was thus like drawing a gun; whoever did so first enjoyed a huge strategic advantage. But, if Russia did not do so first, her administrative backwardness and the vast distances her reservists had to travel would put her at an equally huge disadvantage with respect to the more compact and better-organized Germany. In fact, neither for her nor for her French ally did mobilization necessarily mean war, but for Germany mobilization did lead seamlessly into *Aufmarsch*, and *Aufmarsch* into an invasion of Belgium timetabled to the last minute. Russian mobilization gave her the excuse. Last-minute attempts by a panic-stricken Kaiser to delay matters were useless. The order to mobilize was given in Berlin on 1 August. An ultimatum demanding free passage through Belgium was issued the following day, and when

2 Belgian refugees: the first fruits of the German invasion

it was rejected German troops crossed the frontier on 3 August.

In Britain the invasion of Belgium united what had until then been a deeply divided public opinion. Ever since the sixteenth century it had been an article of faith in British naval policy that the Low Countries should not be allowed to fall into hostile hands, and this belief had become almost visceral, irrespective of party politics. The British government at once issued an ultimatum demanding assurances that Belgian neutrality would be respected. It remained unanswered, and Britain declared war on Germany on 4 August. Liberal concerns for the rights of small nations combined with traditional conservative concern for the maintenance of the balance of European power to make parliamentary support almost unanimous. A state of war was proclaimed throughout the British Empire and the 'First World War' began.

# 3

# 1914: The Opening Campaigns

## *Popular Reactions*

The outbreak of war was greeted with enthusiasm in the major cities of all the belligerent powers, but this urban excitement was not necessarily typical of public opinion as a whole. The mood in France in particular was one of stoical resignation—one that probably characterized all agrarian workers who were called up and had to leave their land to be cultivated by women and children. But everywhere peoples were supportive of their governments. This was no 'limited war' between princely states. War was now a national affair. For a century past, national self-consciousness had been inculcated by state educational programmes directed to forming loyal and obedient citizens. Indeed, as societies became increasingly secular, the concept of the Nation, with all its military panoply and heritage, acquired a quasi-religious significance. Conscription assisted this indoctrination process but was not essential to it: public opinion in Britain, where conscription was not introduced until 1916, was as keenly nationalistic as anywhere on the Continent. For thinkers saturated in Darwinian theory, war was seen as a test of 'manhood' such as soft urban living no longer afforded. Such 'manhood' was believed to be essential if nations were to be 'fit to survive' in a world where progress was the result, or so they believed, of competition rather than cooperation, between nations as between species. Liberal pacifism remained influential in Western democracies, but it was also widely seen, especially in Germany, as a symptom of moral decadence.

Such sophisticated belligerence made the advent of war welcome to many intellectuals, as well as to members of the old ruling classes, who accepted with enthusiasm their traditional function of leadership in war. Artists, musicians, academics, and writers vied with each other in offering their services to their governments. For artists in particular, Futurists in Italy, Cubists in France, Vorticists in Britain, Expressionists in Germany, war was seen as an aspect of the liberation from an outworn regime that they themselves had been pioneering for a decade past. Workers in urban environments looked forward to finding in it an exciting and, they hoped, a brief respite from the tedium of their everyday lives. In the democracies of Western Europe mass opinion, reinforced by government propaganda, swept along the less enthusiastic. In the less literate and developed societies further east, traditional feudal loyalty, powerfully reinforced by religious sanctions, was equally effective in mass mobilization.

And it must be remembered that all governments could make out a plausible case. The Austrians were fighting for the preservation of their historic multinational empire against disintegration provoked by their old adversary Russia. The Russians were fighting for the protection of their Slav kith and kin, for the defence of their national honour, and to fulfil their obligations to their ally France. The French were fighting in self-defence against totally unprovoked aggression by their traditional enemy. The British were fighting to uphold the law of nations and to pre-empt the greatest threat they had faced from the Continent since the days of Napoleon. The Germans were fighting on behalf of their one remaining ally, and to repel a Slavic threat from the east that had joined forces with their jealous rivals in the west to stifle their rightful emergence as a World Power. These were the arguments that governments presented to their peoples. But the peoples did not have to be whipped up by government propaganda. It was in a spirit of simple patriotic duty that they joined the colours and went to war.

Writing at the end of the nineteenth century the German military writer Colmar von der Goltz had warned that any future European war would see 'an exodus of nations', and he was proved right. In August 1914 the armies of Europe mobilized some six million men and hurled them against their neighbours. German armies invaded France and Belgium. Russian armies invaded Germany. Austrian armies invaded Serbia and Russia. French armies attacked over the frontier into German Alsace-Lorraine. The British sent an expeditionary force to help the French, confidently expecting to reach Berlin by Christmas. Only the Italians, whose obligations under the Triple Alliance covered only a defensive war and ruled out incurring British hostility, prudently waited on events. If 'the Allies' (as the Franco-Russo-British alliance became generally known) won, Italy might gain the lands she claimed from Austria; if 'the Central Powers' (the Austro-Germans), she might win not only the contested

borderlands with France, Nice and Savoy, but French possessions in North Africa to add to the Mediterranean empire she
had already begun to acquire at the expense of the Turks.
Italy's policy was guided, as their Prime Minister declared
with endearing frankness, by *sacro egoismo*.

## The Invasion of Belgium

We have seen how the military plans of all the belligerents
were based on the assumption that, if the war were not to be
disastrous, it had to be kept short, and that a successful offensive was the only way to ensure that it was. Nowhere was this
believed more strongly than in Berlin. The General Staff had
calculated that the French army had to be defeated within six
weeks if sufficient forces were to be transferred to meet and
defeat the expected Russian attack in the east. That could be
done only by the great outflanking movement through Belgium visualized by Schlieffen—a manœuvre aimed not only
at defeating the French armies but at surrounding and
annihilating them in a *Schlacht ohne Morgen*—'a battle without
a tomorrow'. Schlieffen's successor, Helmuth von Moltke,
nephew of the great field marshal who had led Prussian
forces to victory in 1866 and 1870, modified the plan so as to
provide better protection against a possible French invasion
of south Germany and to avoid having to invade Holland as
well; for, if the war did drag on, a neutral Holland would be
essential for the German economy. After the war Moltke was
accused of having ruined Schlieffen's concept, but later
research has shown Schlieffen's recommendations to have
been logistically impossible. A German invasion of Belgium

had been generally expected—the railheads constructed along the Belgian frontier gave the game away—but French and British staff calculations had concluded that constraints both of logistics and of manpower would confine the movement to the right bank of the Meuse. It was only the two additional army corps provided by the German military reforms of 1911–12, and the unorthodox use of reservist units as front-line troops, that enabled Moltke to flesh out Schlieffen's ideas, and mount an attack on a scale that took the Allies completely by surprise.

The Belgians had prepared for a German invasion by constructing a major fortification complex at Liège. To deal with this the Germans employed their major 'secret weapon'— mobile siege artillery, especially heavy howitzers from the Austrian Skoda works, whose shells crashed through steel and concrete and battered the garrison into surrender. By 17 August they had cleared the way, and the German march through Belgium began. Before them the German armies drove a flood of refugees who clogged the roads with carts bearing all that they could rescue of their possessions—the first trickle of that immense and miserable flood of uprooted humanity that was to characterize warfare for the rest of the century. Those who remained were treated by the invaders with a harshness intended to pre-empt the kind of 'people's war' of sabotage and assassination that the French had begun to wage against their invaders in 1870. Seeing saboteurs and *francs-tireurs* even when they did not exist, German troops took and shot an estimated 5,000 Belgian civilians and indiscriminately set fire to buildings, including those of the medieval university of Louvain. Wildly exaggerated reports of their atrocities were spread in Britain, confirming public support for a war that rapidly came to be seen as a crusade against barbaric German militarism—a view that spread to influential quarters in the United States. If the invasion itself had not been enough to provoke Britain to intervene, the manner in which the German forces enforced their occupation would have created almost irresistible pressure to do so.

### The Battle of the Marne

Meanwhile General Joseph Joffre, the French commander-in-chief, launched his own offensive further south—initially into Alsace-Lorraine, largely to satisfy public opinion, then northward into the flank of the German attack. Everywhere French forces were repulsed with heavy losses, largely in encounter battles with the advancing Germans whose heavy artillery often destroyed French units long before they could bring their own lighter guns to bear. The French armies were thus already falling back when the German outflanking movement began to take effect. The right wing of the German forces, General von Kluck's First Army, passed through Brussels on 20 August and two days later found the Allied left flank in the industrial town of Mons. There the two corps of the British Expeditionary Force under Field Marshal Sir John French had been rushed into the line and had barely taken up their positions when they were attacked. With their French allies on their right, they were forced into a retreat that lasted for two sweltering weeks until, at the beginning of September, the Schlieffen plan came unstuck; the Allies counter-attacked; and the entire German strategy collapsed.

The story of the so-called Battle of the Marne has been retold innumerable times, and everybody involved has claimed the lion's share of the credit. Perhaps the most cogent comment was that of Joffre, who later said that he did not know who had won the battle, but he knew who would have been blamed if it had been lost. Briefly what happened was this. Kluck had been ordered to sweep round to the west and south of Paris in order to encircle and complete the annihilation of the French armies. But on 30 August he decided that, rather than carry out this hugely ambitious operation, he should give priority to maintaining contact with General von Bülow's army on his left, which had been slowed down by French counter-attacks. With Moltke's approval, he therefore deflected his line of advance to the south-east of Paris. Meanwhile Joffre had been using his railway network to switch forces from his right wing to the region of Paris, whence they now threatened Kluck's exposed right flank. On 4 September Joffre halted the retreat of his main forces and simultaneously unleashed this new army against Kluck. When Kluck deployed to meet it, a gap opened between his left flank and Bülow's right, into which British and French forces began to penetrate. Von Moltke, 150 miles behind the front at Luxembourg and receiving only fragmentary messages from his army commanders, became uneasy. He had already weakened his forces by sending two army corps to the Eastern Front, where things seemed to be going badly wrong. On 8 September he sent his Chief of Intelligence, Colonel Hentsch, to see what was happening, with plenipotentiary powers to sort matters out. Hentsch found both army headquarters in a state of confusion, and confirmed their own inclination to retreat. The whole

German line fell back to the line of the Aisne, the French and British cautiously following. There the Germans established themselves in positions that they were successfully to defend for the best part of four years to come.

## The First Battle of Ypres

Moltke, an unstable character at the best of times, now suffered a nervous collapse, and was replaced in command of the German armies by the Minister for War, Erich von Falkenhayn. Falkenhayn knew as well as anyone the importance of gaining victory before winter set in. He rushed every unit he could lay hands on to rescue what he could of the Schlieffen plan by outflanking the Allies to the north. Joffre responded in kind, placing the northern section of the front under the command of the most inspiring of his subordinate commanders, General Ferdinand Foch. The coast was held by all that was left of the Belgian army, which had made a brief stand at Antwerp, gallantly if ineffectually assisted by a scratch relief force from Britain, before having to fall back on 6 October. The British Expeditionary Force, now three corps strong, just had time to take up positions on the right of the Belgians around Ypres before, on 30 October, the German attack began.

Both sides knew that this might be the decisive battle of the war. The British had put into the line virtually the whole of their old regular army, whose quality more than compensated for its diminutive size. Falkenhayn attacked with four newly created army corps, some units of which consisted largely of untrained students below military age. They attacked with desperate courage, to be mown down in their thousands by British rifles and machine guns outside the village of Langemarck in what became known in Germany as the *Kindermord*, the 'Massacre of the Innocents'. But the British line just held, and on 11 November beat off the last German attack.

The First Battle of Ypres, as it came to be called, saw the end of the old British army. It also saw the end of mobile war on the Western Front. The trenches hastily scrabbled in the boggy soil round Ypres became part of a line stretching from the North Sea to the Swiss frontier that was, as we have seen, to remain essentially unchanged for four more terrible years.

## *The Eastern Front in 1914*

On the Eastern Front the situation was a great deal more confused. Political logic would have led the Austrians to concentrate their attack on Serbia, the original occasion for the war, and the Russians to advance south as quickly as possible to rescue the Serbs. It did not work out like that. Both governments had divided purposes. The Russian government was certainly under strong pressure to help the Serbs, mainly from the Panslav nationalists who had for fifty years past been the driving force behind Russian expansion in the Balkans. But there was equally strong pressure to help the French from the liberal bourgeoisie whose ties with the West had been cemented by French loans and investments. There was also a significant pro-German faction, especially among the court aristocracy, that had been momentarily silenced but was to become increasingly powerful as the war went on. The

High Command was riven by political and professional rivalries that the Czar tried to resolve by creating two totally separate army groups under the nominal command of his uncle the Grand Duke Nicholas. These were to fight separate wars, one in the north-west in Poland and East Prussia against Germany, the other in the south in Galicia against Austria-Hungary.

Ever since 1911, when the great increases in the German army began, the French High Command had been urging on the Russians the need for a rapid attack to distract as many German forces as possible from the offensive in the west. The Russian northern army group did its best. On 15 August, while the German forces in the west were still held up by the forts of Liège, the Russian First Army under General Rennenkampf drove into East Prussia from the east, and five days later inflicted a sharp reverse on the Germans at Gumbinnen. On the same day the Second Army under General Samsonov advanced from the south, threatening the German right flank. The German concentration against France had left only one army to defend the eastern frontier. Its commander, General von Prittwitz, panicked and ordered a general withdrawal behind the Vistula.

But East Prussia, the historic heartland of the Prussian monarchy, could not be so easily abandoned. Prittwitz was dismissed, to be replaced by the formidable combination of Paul von Hindenburg and Erich Ludendorff. Hindenburg, a solid embodiment of the traditional Prussian virtues, had served in the wars of both 1866 and 1870 and had been recalled from retirement at the age of 66. Ludendorff, his Chief of Staff, was a middle-class professional whose ferocious competence had been displayed as much in the bureaucratic battles over the expansion of the army before the war as by his astounding performance in its early days when he had driven in a commandeered car between the outlying forts into Liège and bluffed the authorities into surrendering the central citadel. On their arrival they adopted a plan already prepared by Prittwitz's equally able Chief of Staff Colonel Max Hoffmann, whereby only a thin cavalry screen was left to delay Rennenkampf's advance from the east while the bulk of German forces was concentrated against Samsonov. The success of this manœuvre owed much to German foreknowledge of Russian plans gleaned from reading their radio signals dispatched *en clair*, and more to the initiative of a German corps commander, General von François, who ignored orders to stand fast and boldly advanced to cut off Samsonov's retreat to the south. The three-day battle of Tannenberg (27–30 August) resulted in 50,000 Russians killed or wounded and 90,000 prisoners. It was one of the greatest military victories of all time and has been studied in staff colleges ever since, but its effect on the outcome of the war was negligible. Its only lasting result was the elevation of Hindenburg and Ludendorff in Germany to the status of demigods. In the subsequent fighting among the Masurian lakes the Germans took a further 30,000 prisoners, but lost 100,000 men of their own.

Further south the Austrians, like the Russians, were divided in purpose. The distinct preference of their Chief of Staff, Conrad von Hötzendorf, was to deal once and for all with the troublesome Serbs, but he had four Russian armies massing against him on the frontiers of Galicia and was receiving daily messages from Berlin urging him to engage them and relieve pressure on the German army. Conrad made the worst of both worlds. His attack on Serbia went off at half-cock. The Serbs were hardened fighters who drove the Austrians back across their frontier with the loss of 30,000 men. His attack northward into Russian Poland resulted in confused encounter battles, until ultimately a Russian threat to his right flank forced him to fall back to the Carpathians, abandoning the key fortress of Przemysl and losing a further 350,000 men. The Germans responded to his increasingly desperate cries for help by attacking over the western frontier of Poland towards Warsaw. In November, while the British were fighting at Ypres, huge and inconclusive battles were swirling around Lodz, in which each side lost about 100,000 men. The irrepressible Conrad then launched a winter offensive across the Carpathians to relieve Przemysl. This collapsed in howling snowstorms, and Przemysl surrendered the following March. By then the Habsburg army had lost over two million men.

So by the end of 1914 the short war for which Europe's armies had been preparing for the previous forty years was over; but nobody had won it.

# 4

# 1915: The War Continues

Had this been a 'limited war' in the style of the eighteenth century, governments might at this point have declared a truce and patched up a compromise peace. Left to themselves, the original protagonists, Russia and Austria-Hungary, would almost certainly have done so. But the original causes of the war were now almost forgotten, and what those powers felt hardly mattered. Their allies were now in the driving seat, and had no intention of calling a halt. The German armies after a succession of brilliant successes were deep inside the territory of their adversaries, and were confident that they could complete their victory during the coming year. Their government had already drafted, in the so-called September Programme, the peace terms they intended to impose on their defeated enemies. In the west, Belgium would become a German protectorate. France would be made to yield yet more land on her eastern borders and demilitarize her northern territories as far south as the mouth of the Somme. In the east, German frontiers would be pushed deep into Poland and extended north along the Baltic littoral. Heavy indemnities would be demanded from the defeated Allies, commensurate with

3  Germany's self-image during the war

Germany's own losses of 'blood and treasure'. For France, naturally enough, there could be no peace so long as the German army occupied a fifth of her most productive territory. As for opinion in Britain, peace was unthinkable so long as Germany continued to occupy and behave so outrageously in Belgium, and the million or so men who had voluntarily enlisted on the outbreak of the war had barely begun to fight.

In any case for both sides, especially for Britain and Germany, the war was no longer just a traditional struggle for power, but increasingly a conflict of ideologies. If conservatives in Britain saw it as a defence of the British Empire against the challenge of a rival Great Power, liberals saw it as a struggle for democracy and the rule of law against the jackboot of Prussian militarism, whose treatment of Belgium gave a foretaste of what Europe had to expect at the hands of a victorious Germany. The demonization of Germany was, of

4 The image of Germany in Allied propaganda

course, to be intensified by official propaganda, but that did no more than play on emotions already being ventilated and intensified by the press. The degree of popular hysteria was such that even the most distinguished families with German names found it convenient to relabel themselves: the Battenbergs as Mountbatten, the Royal family itself (generally known as the House of Hanover but more accurately Saxe-Coburg-Gotha) as the House of Windsor. At the lower end of the animal scale, the popular breed of German sheepdogs was rebranded as 'Alsatians', and dachshunds disappeared from the streets. Wagner's music was effectively banned. In Germany reactions were no less intense. The antagonism found expression in Ernst Lissauer's popular *Hassgesang*, a Hymn of Hate, which indicted England as Germany's most dangerous and treacherous foe. German academics and intellectuals joined forces to depict Germany as fighting for a unique *Kultur* against Slavic barbarism on the one hand, and, on the other, the frivolity and decadence of French *civilisation* and the brutish shopkeepers' materialism of the Anglo-Saxons—a *Kultur* that embodied and was defended by the warrior virtues that the West condemned as militaristic. Such 'popular passions' were at least as important as political or military calculations in the determination of the belligerents to press on with the war.

### War at Sea

The British government had initially shared the continental illusion that the war would be ended in a matter of months—not through a military decision but from a collapse of the financial system that enabled the economy of the belligerent powers to function at all. There was general surprise when the incoming Secretary of State for War, Britain's most distinguished living soldier Lord Kitchener, warned his civilian colleagues to plan for a war lasting for at least three years, but historical precedent gave no reason to suppose that it would be over any more quickly. Even if Germany were as successful by land as had been Napoleon, the war was likely to go on as it had in the days of Napoleon; and, like Napoleon, Germany would ultimately be defeated by British 'command of the sea'. The main concern of the Royal Navy was to ensure that this would be the case.

About the importance of that 'command' no one was in any doubt. Orthodox naval opinion, in Germany as well as in Britain, believed that it was won or lost by a clash of great battle fleets, as it had been in the age of Nelson. The victor would then be able to starve his opponent into surrender, or at least so disrupt his trade that his economy would collapse and he would no longer be able to continue the war. In spite of Tirpitz's building programme, the German High Seas Fleet was still in no position to challenge the British Grand Fleet; but the British were too wary of the lethal power of mines and torpedoes to seek out the German fleet in its North Sea bases or impose a close blockade on the German coast. Their caution appeared justified when on 22 September 1914 a German submarine sank three British cruisers in the English Channel, with a loss of 1,500 lives. The Grand Fleet therefore remained in harbour at Scapa Flow, in the extreme north of Scotland, watching in case the German fleet attempted a sortie. Its opponents in the German High Seas Fleet did the same, while the Royal Navy swept German shipping from the seas. The few German commerce-raiders at sea when war broke out were quickly hunted down, though not before a squadron under Admiral Graf von Spee destroyed a British detachment at Coronel off the coast of Chile on 1 November 1914—to be destroyed in its turn in the Battle of the Falkland Islands a month later.

German cruisers bombarded English coastal towns during the winter of 1914–15, and there was a clash on the Dogger Bank in January, but otherwise both fleets remained inactive. After two years a new German commander, Admiral Scheer, lost patience. On 31 May 1916 he led the High Seas Fleet out into the North Sea to challenge the Grand Fleet to battle. The British took up the challenge, and the two fleets clashed off the Danish coast in what for the British became known as the Battle of Jutland, for the Germans as that of the Skaggerak. The unprecedented nature of the encounter and the failure of signal communications made the battle itself inconclusive. The Germans sank fourteen British ships totalling 110,000 tons as against their own loss of eleven ships totalling 62,000 tons, and so were able plausibly to claim a tactical victory. But the strategic situation remained unchanged. British ships continued to dominate the world's oceans, and the German High Seas Fleet to rot in harbour until the end of the war.

### Colonial Warfare

'Command of the sea' also meant that Germany was cut off from her colonies, but these were too few to matter. Unlike the French in the eighteenth century, whose colonies had been a major source of wealth that could be transferred to their conqueror, the Germans had acquired overseas colonies mainly for reasons of prestige, to bolster their claim to the status of *Weltmacht*; but they were if anything a drain on their economy. Their islands in the Central Pacific—the Marshalls, the Marianas, the Carolines—were quickly seized by Britain's allies the Japanese, as was their base Tsingtao on the Chinese mainland. Those in the South Pacific—Samoa, Papua, the Solomons, the Bismarcks—were taken by the Australians and New Zealanders. Ironically, although all were to be the scenes of desperate fighting in the Second World War, in the First they hardly rated as sideshows. In West Africa, French and British colonial troops cooperated in clearing Togoland and the German Cameroons. South African forces, largely Boers who had been fighting the British fifteen years earlier, captured German South-West Africa, later Namibia, but German East Africa, later Tanzania, proved a very much harder nut to crack. The commander of the garrison, Paul von Lettow-Vorbeck, first repulsed a landing by Anglo-Indian troops at Tanga, and then evaded and harassed an expedition sent to destroy him under one of the stars of the Boer War, Jan Christian Smuts, in a guerrilla campaign that was still being successfully waged when the war ended in Europe in 1918.

Lettow-Vorbeck brilliantly upheld the honour of German arms, but the effect of his campaign on the outcome of the war was negligible. It was clear from the outset that the war would be decided on European battlefields. Although the British had been laying plans for 'Imperial Defence' for the previous thirty years, these had been concerned not so much with the defence of imperial territory overseas as with contributions from the Empire to the Royal Navy, and with the homogenization of Canadian, Australian, and New Zealand forces with those of the United Kingdom. British command of the seas enabled those forces to be brought to Europe, some of them escorted by Japanese warships. All were volunteers. Many were first-generation immigrants or their children for whom Britain was still 'home', and membership of the British Empire a cause for pride. In addition, détente with Russia had freed the Indian army for service overseas, although the miserable winter of 1914 that many of them spent in the waterlogged trenches of the Western Front made it clear that this was not the best way to use their services. Fortunately a more convenient theatre of war opened up for them when, at the end of October, the Ottoman Empire entered the war at the side of Germany.

### The Dardanelles and Salonica Campaigns

The Ottoman Empire ('Turkey' for short) was a major actor on the European scene whose role we have not yet considered. After a century of degeneracy, defeat, and humiliation, when she survived mainly because the European powers saw her existence as necessary to preserve the balance in Eastern Europe, power had been seized in 1908 by a group of young officers (the original 'Young Turks') set on modernizing the archaic political and economic system and restoring national prestige. They turned their backs on the Islamic traditions of the Ottoman Empire with its vast sprawling frontiers in Africa and Arabia in favour of a compact ethnically homogeneous Turkey that would eliminate alien elements—Greek, Armenian—within her own territory and sponsor a Pan-Turanian movement that would liberate and unite the thirty million ethnic Turks of the Caucasus, southern Russia, and Central Asia under a single rule. The Russians viewed the advent of this new regime with understandable alarm, the more so since in Germany it found enthusiastic support. German investment poured into the country, especially for the development of its railways. German diplomats exercised the commanding influence in Constantinople that had been a British prerogative in the previous century, while German officers assisted in the training and re-equipment of the Turkish army—though not in time to save it from humiliating defeat in the First Balkan War of 1912. There is still a special shrine in honour of its German mentors in the Turkish Army Museum in Istanbul.

The British took a relaxed view of all this. Once they had established themselves in Egypt in the 1880s, they had abandoned the thankless task of propping up the Turks as a barrier to Russian expansion. Indeed, they initially saw in the German presence there a useful counterweight against Russia. When Russia became an ally, the Straits linking the Mediterranean with the Black Sea, through which passed a third of all Russian exports, acquired a new strategic importance, but it was assumed that Anglo-French command of the Mediterranean would be enough to ensure safe passage. Further, if the Germans controlled the Turkish army, the British were equally influential in the Turkish navy. Two state-of-the-art battleships had been built for it in British yards, and in August 1914 they were ready for delivery. But when war broke out the British government stepped in and purchased the ships for themselves, thus alienating their chief supporters in Constantinople. Admittedly the Turks had just concluded a treaty with Germany directed against the Russians, so there could be no guarantee that the vessels would not fall under German control; and the incident might have been forgotten if two German warships, the *Goeben* and the *Breslau*, had not successfully evaded British pursuit in the Mediterranean on the outbreak of war and cast anchor off Constantinople on 12 August. Their brooding presence, combined with the stunning successes of the German armies on all fronts, helped persuade the Turkish government to declare war on Russia, and on 29 October the German ships, now flying the Turkish flag, bombarded the Black Sea port of Odessa. At the same time the Turks took the offensive against the Russians by attacking in that historic arena of Russo-Turkish conflict, the Caucasus—an unwise thing to do at the onset of winter, as the 80,000 Turkish losses during the next three months were to testify.

The British did not lament this diplomatic defeat, and may indeed have deliberately courted it. The decrepit Ottoman Empire was more useful to them as a victim than as a dependent ally. The Colonial Office and the India Office had long seen Turkey's Asian possessions as a legitimate prey for the British Empire. The Royal Navy, having recently begun to convert from coal to oil-burning ships, had its eyes on the oil refineries at Basra at the head of the Persian Gulf. With Turkey as an enemy, Britain could now convert her anomalous occupation of Egypt into a full protectorate. London even felt self-confident enough to promise Constantinople, seen for 100 years past as a bastion of British security, to their new allies the Russians. It was still assumed that Turkey, with her political life concentrated in Constantinople, would be easily vulnerable to the pressure of British sea power. All that was needed was to force a passage through the Dardanelles, which nobody thought would be very difficult; and early in 1915 preparations were made to do just that.

The Dardanelles campaign was triggered in January 1915 by a request from the hard-pressed Russians for a 'demonstration' against Constantinople to relieve Turkish pressure in the Caucasus. There were influential forces in Whitehall that had always questioned the wisdom of committing the British army to a land campaign in Western Europe instead of using Britain's maritime power to blockade the enemy and her financial strength to support continental allies—the strategy that had served them so well in the Napoleonic Wars. Now they had their chance—especially since the army had failed to secure the decision on the Western Front that had been so confidently expected. The young First Lord of the Admiralty, Winston Churchill, urged on the Dardanelles expedition with his incomparable eloquence. His colleague at the War Office, Lord Kitchener, an imperial soldier who had spent most of his life in the Middle East, favoured it as well. For one thing it would reopen communications with Russia, freeing her to export the grain that played so vital a part in her economy. For another, a 'back door' could be opened through the Balkans to help the Serbs, who were still successfully resisting Austrian attack; and Serbia's former allies of the Balkan Wars, Bulgaria and Greece, might be persuaded to come to her help as well. Bulgaria, admittedly, was a very long shot. Traditionally hostile to Serbia anyway, she had lost to her in the Second Balkan War the lands in Macedonia that she saw as her rightful reward for her efforts in the First, and was longing to get them back. The Allies hoped to compensate her at the expense of Austria-Hungary, but the Central Powers were in a far stronger position to woo her, both diplomatically and militarily. No one was very surprised when Bulgaria entered the war on the side of the Central Powers in October 1915.

But Greece was a different matter. She had been Serbia's ally in both Balkan Wars. Her business and trading classes were strongly anglophile. The army and court were equally strongly pro-German—not surprisingly, given that the King was the Kaiser's brother-in-law (most of the new Balkan states had gone shopping for their royal families in Germany). The Prime Minister, Eleutherios Venizelos, a Cretan, was himself a strong supporter of the Allies, but demanded a high price for Greek support—Constantinople, which had unfortunately already been promised to the Russians. Nevertheless the Serb victories over the Austrians in the winter of 1914 and the Allied landings at the Dardanelles the following March strengthened his hand sufficiently for him to accept an Allied request (largely inspired by the French) that they should land a small army at Salonica to bring direct help to the Serbs. This force landed in October 1915.

By then a great deal had happened. The Dardanelles expedition had failed. Its military objectives had from the beginning been confused. The Royal Navy had been ordered simply 'to bombard and take the Gallipoli peninsula, with Constantinople as its objective'. But when they attacked in March 1915, Allied (Anglo-French) naval forces had been turned back by enemy minefields, and had called in land forces to help. Troops were then committed piecemeal to the Gallipoli peninsula, had suffered heavy losses in landing, and could then only cling on to narrow beachheads overlooked by strong Turkish defences. A major British attack in August at Suvla Bay failed owing to the incompetence of its commanders. By October it was clear that the operation had been a total failure, redeemed only by the courage and endurance of the troops, especially those from Australia and New Zealand, who had carried it out, and by the successful evacuation of the peninsula at the end of the year. The Allies had thus lost all credit in the eastern Mediterranean. In Greece, Venizelos was disgraced; and, when the Allied expedition eventually landed at Salonica, the new Greek government complained bitterly of the infringement of its neutrality—which was especially embarrassing for the British liberals who claimed to be fighting for the rights of small nations.

To make matters worse, the Central Powers had taken the military initiative in the Balkans with far greater success. In November 1915 Austrian and German forces under German command, joined by Bulgarians, invaded Serbia from three sides, pre-empting the Allied advance from Salonica to help her. Serbia was crushed and occupied, the remnants of her defeated army straggling over the Montenegrin mountains in mid-winter to escape through the Adriatic ports. Those who survived joined the Allied force at Salonica, which was left in a state of almost comic impotence, while the Austrians were now able to concentrate their strength on their preferred adversaries; the Italians.

### *Italy Enters the War*

Italy, as we have seen, had declared her neutrality when war broke out. There was no great enthusiasm for joining in the war: the Treasury had been drained by the war against the Turks, and industry was paralysed by strikes. The Church and much of the aristocracy favoured the cause of the Catholic Austrians against the liberal West. But the traditions of the *Risorgimento,* the prospect of the final unification of the Italian nation, gave the Allied cause a great popular advantage, which the Central Powers could match only by ceding the Italian-speaking territories still in Austrian possession. The Germans brought heavy pressure to bear on their Austrian allies to do this, but Vienna was understandably reluctant. After all, the war was being fought to preserve the Monarchy, not to dismantle it. The Italians were universally unpopular, besides being the only adversaries the Austrians were confident of being able to defeat. Nevertheless, in May 1915 Vienna reluctantly yielded to German pressure. It was too late: the Italians had signed the secret Treaty of London with the Allies on 26 April. By this they were promised all the Italian-speaking regions south of the Alps, together with wide areas of Slovenia and Dalmatia where the Italians were in a definite minority—to say nothing of a substantial share in Turkish Anatolia where there were no Italians at all.

Italy declared war on 23 May 1915, and her commander-in-chief General Luigi Cadorna spent the next two years launching suicidal attacks in the mountains beyond the Isonzo, losing almost a million men in the process. The Austrian army fought them with an enthusiasm that it had shown on no other front. Arguably, the Italian entry into the war did more for the morale of the Austrian army than the victories it had won, very much as a junior partner to the Germans, over the Serbs and Russians in the course of 1915. Certainly it did little to compensate the Allies for the loss of the Balkans and their defeat at the hands of the Turks.

## The Eastern Front in 1915

Nor had the Allies done any better on their major fronts. The strategic initiative still lay with Berlin—in particular with Erich von Falkenhayn, the highly competent new Chief of the General Staff. Falkenhayn had a clear order of priorities. He realized that Germany's most dangerous enemies lay in the west. Unless France and, even more important, Britain, were defeated, the Allies could prolong the war indefinitely—not so much through their own military strength as through the maritime superiority that enabled them to draw on the economic resources of the New World and deny them to Germany. Russia no longer presented any immediate threat, and the sheer size of the eastern theatre made it difficult to obtain a decisive victory on that front. Left to himself, Falkenhayn would have returned to the Schlieffen strategy of allocating minimal forces to hold the Russians while concentrating everything on securing a decisive victory in the west. But he was not left to himself. For the German public the great heroes of the war were now the victors of Tannenberg: Hindenburg and Ludendorff. This formidable couple had no intention of allowing their theatre to dwindle into a backwater, and they now commanded enough political influence to ensure that it did not. Moreover, the Austrians at the end of their disastrous winter campaign were on the verge of collapse. Already by the end of 1914 they had lost a million and a quarter men. By March they had lost a further

5 German troops burning a village on the Eastern Front

800,000. Those losses included most of the professional cadres that had held the multinational army together, and Slav units—Czech, Romanian, and Ruthene—were beginning to desert *en masse*. Conrad himself began to consider a separate peace with Russia, if only to deal with the Italians more effectively.

Reluctantly, therefore, Falkenhayn accepted that for the time being he would have to stand on the defensive in the west and attack strongly enough in the east to rescue his Austrian ally and inflict enough losses on the Russians to strengthen the hand of the influential circles in St Petersburg who were already calling for peace. To this end he created a new Austro-German army group under the command of General August von Mackensen, with Colonel Hans von Seeckt as his Chief of Staff, to attack the Russian positions in Galicia in the region of Gorlice-Tarnow. This offensive saw the first use of the methods that were to characterize the middle years of the war: carefully planned infantry attacks behind a curtain of prolonged and concentrated artillery fire. It was a total success: 100,000 prisoners were taken and the Russian lines penetrated to a depth of eighty miles. It was not in itself 'decisive', but for Falkenhayn that was not the point. He was beginning to understand the nature of this new kind of warfare. In this, the object was not victory in the field so much as 'attrition'. Germany's strategy should now be to compel her adversaries to exhaust their resources while committing as few as possible of her own.

Hindenburg and Ludendorff disagreed. They still visualized a far-reaching strategy of encirclement that would trap the entire Russian army, as Schlieffen had hoped to encircle the French, in 'a battle without a tomorrow'. Falkenhayn would have none of this. In August he authorized an offensive in the northern sector of the front, but with the limited objective of driving the Russians out of Poland and establishing a defensive line running north–south through Brest-Litovsk. This operation was so successful that he then allowed Ludendorff to carry out a further sweeping advance in the north to take Vilna; but, once again, the German army secured a spectacular operational victory that had no strategic consequence.

By the end of 1915 the German record on the Eastern Front had been one of unbroken success, for which Hindenburg and Ludendorff reaped the credit. But these brilliant victories over greatly superior forces owed little to skilful generalship. They were due rather to good organization, superior logistics, better training, and better intelligence, much of it gained electronically through listening to Russian messages transmitted *en clair*; qualities possessed in abundance by a highly educated and industrious people whose development was still far ahead of the Russian Empire.

Also significant, however, was the brutality with which this campaign was conducted on both sides, of which civilians were the chief victims. Russian troops devastated the countryside as they withdrew, having no fellow feeling for its Polish and Lithuanian inhabitants. The number of refugees was estimated at between three million and ten million. The Germans were even less concerned with civilian welfare. They advanced not only as conquerors but as colonizers: this was territory that Ludendorff planned to annex as part of a greater Reich, settled and dominated by Germans. The region became known simply as OberOst, after the military organization that ruled it. German officials treated the inhabitants as barbarians, without rights or identity of their own. In this, as in so many other respects, German actions in the First World War grimly foreshadowed their behaviour in the Second.

## The Western Front in 1915

On the Western Front the Germans stood on the defensive throughout 1915, and were equally successful. They attacked only once, at Ypres in April, with little serious strategic purpose other than to try out a new weapon, chlorine poison gas. Initially this was highly effective: the Allied troops against whom it was deployed, taken completely by surprise, temporarily abandoned an 8,000-yard stretch of the front line. But the Allies rapidly improvised antidotes and embodied the weapon in their own arsenals, making the conduct of the war yet more complex and inhumane. Since this new 'frightfulness' was added to the German record of barbarism and was to be one of the most valuable items of Allied propaganda both during and after the war, more was probably lost than gained by this innovation. For the rest, the German armies perfected their defensive positions, usually on ground of their own choosing—digging systems of trenches with deep and often comfortable dug-outs, protected by barbed-wire entanglements and defended not only by pre-registered artillery but by machine guns, which now came into their own in the kind of defensive warfare that no European army had expected to have to fight.

These defences the Allied armies felt compelled to attack. For one thing, they lay deep inside French territory, and for the French at least it was unthinkable that they should remain there unchallenged. For another, the disasters on the Eastern Front made continuing pressure in the west appear essential if the Russians were to be kept in the war at all. Strategic direction was still largely in the hands of the French, with the British very much as junior partners. There was still heavy pressure within the British Cabinet in favour of limiting the British contribution on the Western Front and seeking a more traditional maritime strategy—a view to which Kitchener himself was strongly sympathetic. Even the most enthusiastic 'westerners', as they came to be called, would have preferred to delay any offensive until 1916, when they hoped that their new armies would be properly trained and equipped. But the failure of the Dardanelles campaign, the pressure of their allies, and above all the weight of a public opinion anxious to come to grips with the Germans, meant that by the end of 1915 the British were irrevocably committed to a 'western' strategy, and looked forward to its consummation the following year.

So throughout 1915, in a succession of attacks of increasing intensity, the French and British armies learned the techniques of the new kind of war at very heavy cost. Their early attacks in March were easily repulsed. It became obvious that the key to a successful assault lay in sufficient artillery support, but the Allied armies did not as yet have either enough guns of the right calibre or the industry capable of manufacturing them, while the guns they did possess did not have the right kind of ammunition. Before 1914 artillery shells had consisted mainly of shrapnel, whose airbursts were effective in mobile warfare. But what was now needed was high explosive, heavy enough to flatten barbed-wire defences, pulverize enemy infantry in their trenches, catch enemy reserves as they moved up to support the defenders, and neutralize enemy artillery by counter-battery fire. Further, infantry attacks had to be carefully coordinated with artillery barrages, which demanded not only first-rate staff work but reliable communications; and the only communications available, in the absence of mobile radio-sets, were runners, carrier pigeons, and telephone lines that were usually the first casualties of an enemy counter-barrage. Finally, even if an attack was initially successful, it could sel-dom penetrate beyond the first line of the German trench system, where it remained vulnerable to bombardment and counter-attack from the flanks. Further advance was then delayed by the need for artillery to re-register its targets. At this stage of the war gunners had to fire 'sighting shots' to ensure accuracy before opening a bombardment. This took time and forfeited surprise. Later (as we shall see) they developed techniques of 'pre-registration' that made this unnecessary. Finally the difficulty of communication between the attacking forces and the reserves needed to complete the breakthrough made command and control on the battlefield almost impossible.

For the British the problem was complicated by the fact that their forces consisted of almost untrained volunteers commanded by officers often promoted far beyond their level of competence; but it must be said that the French, trained as they were for a completely different kind of war-fare, did little better. Nevertheless by September the desper-ate state of the Russians demanded a major effort in the West. The Allies therefore launched a major joint offensive that Joffre promised would 'compel the Germans to retire to the

Meuse and probably end the war'. The British sector centred on the mining region of Loos. The attack was launched with massive artillery support, which now included heavy as well as field guns, and gas was for the first time turned against its inventors. The British indeed actually breached the German

**6** Marshal Joffre with his British junior partners, Field Marshal Sir John French and General Sir Douglas Haig

front line to a width of five miles and a depth of two. But the Germans had also learned lessons, and constructed an entire second defensive position in rear of the first. On the British side faulty staff work, confusion of command, and the sheer friction of war meant that no reserves were on hand to exploit the breach. The operation dragged on for another month, by the end of which both sides had lost some 200,000 men.

None the less the Allies reckoned that they had now found the formula for victory: more guns, longer preliminary barrages, better communications, and better staff work. All this they hoped to put into effect in 1916 in a great joint offensive from east and west planned by the Allied High Command at the French Headquarters at Chantilly in November. Joffre remained securely in the saddle as commander-in-chief of the most powerful allied army in the west, but Britain was becoming an increasingly important partner, as the size of the British Expeditionary Force swelled from its original six to fifty-six divisions, in six armies. It was widely, and rightly, assumed that its commander, Sir John French, was no longer up to the job, and his performance at Loos had proved it. He was replaced by the dour, inarticulate, and iron-willed Sir Douglas Haig; and preparations began for the Battle of the Somme.

# 5

# 1916: The War of Attrition

## *The Home Front*

By the end of 1915 the war that had generally been expected to be over within six months had lasted for nearly a year and a half, and no one any longer expected a rapid conclusion. What had made it possible for it to last so long ?

There is one simple answer: the continuing support of all the belligerent peoples, who not only endured the huge military losses but accepted without complaint the increasing controls and hardships demanded by the conduct of the war. Everywhere governments assumed powers over the lives of their citizens to a degree that was not only unprecedented but had previously been unimaginable. Where governments did not take control, volunteer organizations did. The expected financial collapse at the outbreak of war did not occur. Insurance rates were pegged, government loans were oversubscribed, printed currency replaced gold, labour shortage produced soaring wages, and government contracts created unprecedented prosperity for some sections of the business classes. Agrarian producers suffered severely from shortage of labour, but the demand for their produce was greater than ever. Indeed, after a year of war many sections of the population in all belligerent countries were better off than they had ever been before. But by the end of 1915 the mutual blockade was beginning to bite. Exports declined; prices rose; the inflation resulting from the growing flood of paper money hit the salaried classes; imported raw materials for industry dwindled or disappeared. The combined pressures of the blockade and the demands of the armed forces resulted in growing shortages of food, fuel, and transport; and during 1916 the civilian population began seriously to suffer.

It was the well-organized and cohesive societies of Western Europe—Germany, France, and Britain—that coped best. Indeed, war only made them better organized and more cohesive. The class struggle between capital and labour that had everywhere dominated politics during the first decade of the century was suspended. Labour leaders were given positions of administrative and political responsibility. Labour shortage gave them new bargaining power. Bureaucracies, reinforced by experts from universities and businessmen, took control of more and more aspects of national life, and in many cases were never to lose it. By the end of the war every belligerent European state, even libertarian England, had become a command economy—Germany most of all.

The German, or rather the Prussian, bureaucracy had, like the Prussian army, always been regarded as a model of its kind. It had played little part in preparing for the war: mobilization and everything connected with it were in the hands of the military authorities. There was a good 'war chest' in the *Reichsbank*, but that was as far as civilian war preparations went. In spite of German vulnerability to blockade, nothing had been done to stockpile imported raw materials essential to war production. It was only on the initiative of the civilian Walther Rathenau, creator of the huge electrical combine AEG, that the War Office set up a War Materials Department, initially under his leadership, to control and distribute essential stocks. At the same time the shipping magnate Albert Ballin took the lead in creating a Central Purchasing Organization to rationalize the acquisition of essential imports. Both these organizations were largely run by the businessmen whose activities they controlled. The German chemical industry, the finest in Europe, again took the initiative in developing substitutes (*ersatz*) for unavailable raw materials—wood pulp for textiles, synthetic rubber and nitrates for fertilizer, and explosives synthesized from the atmosphere. Even so, by the end of 1915 both food and clothing were becoming scarce. Rationing and price controls were introduced and generally accepted as fair; but in spite of the victories of their armies, the German people were becoming shabby, anxious, and, in the cities, increasingly hungry.

The British were no better prepared for a prolonged war, but the government had been ready with the initial military and political measures. A 'War Book' had already been prepared giving control over ports, railways, shipping, and insurance rates, and a Defence of the Realm Act was rushed through a unanimous parliament giving the government virtually plenary powers. The government itself, liberal and pacific under the relaxed leadership of Herbert Asquith, initially left the conduct of the war in the hands of Kitchener. Like so many of Britain's military leaders, Kitchener had spent most of his career overseas and was quite out of his depth in the job, but, unlike most of his contemporaries, he realized that the war would be a long one and would need a large army as well as a large navy to fight it. He planned to expand the existing six divisions of the Expeditionary Force to seventy, and appealed for volunteers to fill the ranks. The response was immediate. By the end of 1914 a million men had joined up, far more than could be armed and equipped. But these were less than a quarter of what would ultimately be needed, and by the summer of 1915 the supply of volunteers was drying up. Conscription was anathema to the Liberal government, and a series of half-measures was attempted, until in May 1916 it very reluctantly introduced compulsory military service for all men between 18 and 41.

The place in the workforce of those who joined up was partly filled by women. Women had already been organizing themselves before the war in the 'Suffragette' movement to demand the vote, and the leaders of that movement now swung their influence behind the war effort. Women rapidly became indispensable, not only in the nursing and welfare services but in offices and factories and agriculture, changing the whole balance of society in the process. By 1918 that change was reflected in a new Representation of the People Act, by which the vote was extended from seven million to twenty-one million people, including women over the age of 30. Almost as a by-product of the war, Britain became something approaching a full democracy.

Volunteers and reservists might fill up the ranks of the armed forces, but providing enough weapons and ammunition to arm them was a very different matter. By the end of 1914 practically all the belligerent armies had exhausted

7 Women workers in a munitions factory

their stocks of ammunition, and it was becoming clear that not only men but industry would have to be mobilized for the war effort. In Germany this was done under the auspices of the military, in Britain by the civilians. There the initiative was taken by the most dynamic member of the government, David Lloyd George, who over Kitchener's protests created first a Committee and then in May 1915 a Ministry of Munitions, which combined industry, labour, and civil servants under government control with plenary powers over every aspect of munitions supply. In 1917 further such ministries were created, notably of Food and Shipping, largely staffed by experts from the industries themselves, to handle the problems of rationing that arose from the increasing pressure of blockade. In consequence, although by 1918 much of the population was undernourished, the British never approached the levels of hunger and deprivation that their enemies were to suffer by the end of the war.

France had lost 40 per cent of her coal deposits and 90 per cent of her iron ores to German occupation; but she was still a largely agrarian country, and, although her political leadership was notoriously volatile, her administration was in the hands of the formidably efficient bureaucracy created by Napoleon. More important, she retained access to the resources of the western hemisphere, so her excellent armaments industry did not suffer. Her government, like that of Britain a broad-based coalition of centre and left, initially left the conduct of the war to General Joffre, the hero of the Marne. By the end of 1915 the French army had suffered such terrible losses, and produced so little in the way of results, that doubts were growing about Joffre's competence— doubts that were to be confirmed by his failure to foresee the German offensive against Verdun the following spring. But there was as yet no inclination to make peace. Traditional patriotism of the right, embodied in the president, Raymond Poincaré, united with the bitter Jacobinism of his harshest critic Georges Clemenceau in determination to win the war and destroy Germany's power ever to begin another.

Very different was the situation in the Russian Empire. In spite of her huge manpower and the rapid industrialization of her economy, Russia suffered from two major and ultimately lethal drawbacks: geographical isolation and administrative inefficiency. The first crippled her economy, the second made her incapable of mending it. When war began, essential imports dried up and her export trade—largely grain from southern Russia, blockaded at the Dardanelles—declined by 70 per cent. Domestic production could not fill the gap, although native entrepreneurs made huge profits. The Russian armies, like all the others, rapidly ran out of ammunition—and not only ammunition but guns and even small arms. In the huge battles of 1914–15 Russian infantrymen had to attack unprotected by artillery barrages and often lacking even rifles. Unsurprisingly, by the end of 1915 the Russian army had lost about four million men.

The inability of the slothfully incompetent Russian bureaucracy to remedy the situation led to public outcry and the creation of unofficial councils, Zemstva, first to deal with welfare (including the huge influx of refugees from the war zone) but then with every aspect of war administration—food, fuel, transport, and even military affairs. But, whereas in Western Europe such voluntary agencies were welcomed and used by the government, in Russia their activities were deeply resented—both by the professional bureaucrats themselves, including those in the armed forces, and by the aristocratic clique that dominated the court, led by the Czarina and her sinister adviser the monk Rasputin, who opposed the war anyway. In August 1915 this clique persuaded the Czar to dismiss his uncle Nicolas from command of the armies and take titular command himself. In his absence at headquarters the Czarina was able to take charge of the government and block any further attempts at reform.

The result was tragic. By the beginning of 1916 the efforts of the Zemstva were showing results. There was now an abundance of guns and ammunition, while the High Command had been shaken up and was reaching a new level of competence that was to be revealed by General Brusilov's spectacular success the following summer. But domestically everything was collapsing. The transport system was overwhelmed by the increase in traffic, which led to a breakdown in the supply of fuel and, more important, food for the cities. The winter of 1915–16 saw severe shortage of both in all Russian cities, especially the capital Petrograd (as St Petersburg had been patriotically renamed in 1914). In 1916 the situation was to grow rapidly worse, with growing strikes in the towns and widespread evasion of military service in the countryside. By the end of the year Russia had become ungovernable.

The only consolation for the Allies was that the situation in Austria-Hungary was little better. The Monarchy's only advantage—and it was not always seen as such—was that the Germans could bring direct help. Had this not been so, the Austrians might well have collapsed even sooner than the Russians. The national—or, rather, multinational—solidarity with which the war was greeted did not last. By the spring of 1915, after Conrad's disastrous winter campaign, the Austrian army had lost, as we have seen, over two million men, including the bulk of the professional cadres that had held together a force speaking a dozen native languages. Only increasing infusions of German 'advisers' and staff officers kept it going at all. In domestic affairs the Hungarians increasingly went their own way and, being self-supporting in foodstuffs, suffered little from the prolongation of the war. The Austrians had no such advantage. For food they became dependent on the Hungarians, who were reluctant to provide it. The Austrian economy suffered as much as did the German from the effects of the Allied blockade, but the genially incompetent bureaucracy, fearful of imposing any strain on the doubtful loyalty of its population, barely attempted to plan a siege economy or to administer a rationing system. Vienna began to starve even earlier than Petrograd.

### The Verdun Campaign

By the end of 1915 the German armies had been everywhere victorious, but their victories had brought the end of the war no nearer. The patience of the civilians supporting them was beginning to wear thin. A substantial *fronde* at home, led within the army by Hindenburg and Ludendorff but supported also by Chancellor Bethmann Hollweg, was calling for Falkenhayn's removal. Falkenhayn still retained the confidence of a Kaiser who resented this attempt to usurp his authority, and did not waver in his belief that victory could be won only in the west. With good reason he calculated that his main adversary was no longer a France now nearing exhaustion, but Britain. Britain's armies were still fresh and largely uncommitted, and her command of the seas was not only maintaining the blockade on Germany but keeping open communications with the United States, on whose supplies the Allies were becoming increasingly dependent. To deal with the latter Falkenhayn urged the waging of unrestrained submarine warfare, which we shall consider in due course. On land, however, he believed that Britain's principal weapon was still not her own untried armies, but those of her ally France. If France could be struck such a shattering blow that she was compelled to ask for terms, 'England's sword', as Falkenhayn put it, would be struck from her hand. But, given the tried and tested power of the defensive on the Western Front, how could this be done?

For the solution, Falkenhayn turned to the method that he had already used so successfully in the east: attrition. France should be quite literally bled to death, through the destruction of her armies. The French should be compelled to attack in order to regain territory that they could not afford to lose, and the territory in question would be the fortress of Verdun. Verdun had no strategic importance in itself, but it lay at the apex of a vulnerable salient and was a historic site associated with all the great military glories of France. Falkenhayn reckoned that Joffre could not afford *not* to defend it, or fail to regain it if it were lost. The German armies would inevitably suffer losses in their own attack, but these, he believed, would be minimized by effective use of the techniques used so successfully at Gorlice-Tarnow: surprise, good staff work, and above all massive artillery superiority. So on 21 February 1916, after a nine-hour bombardment with nearly 1,000 guns, the attack began.

Falkenhayn was right. Joffre had regarded Verdun as strategically unimportant and done little to prepare its defence, but political pressure made it impossible for him to abandon it. Under the command of General Philippe Pétain, whose stubborn belief in the power of the defensive had hitherto denied him promotion by his offensively minded superiors, the French troops obeyed their instructions to hang on to every yard of territory, and counter-attack to regain any that was lost. Attrition cut both ways: the French inflicted as many losses as they themselves suffered. Pétain did his best to spare his troops by rotating them, but Falkenhayn had to throw in his men with increasing desperation. It was guns that dominated the battlefield: by the end of June, when the German attacks finally ceased, the artillery of both sides had created a nightmare landscape such as the world had never before seen. To their horror was added that created by gas and flame-throwers in hand-to-hand war. Between them both sides lost half a million men and how many still lie buried in that charnel soil may never be known. Verdun remained in French hands. For the French it was a magnificent victory, but one that had almost shattered their army. For the Germans it was their first undeniable setback, a heavy blow to the morale of both army and people, and Falkenhayn paid the price. In August he was relieved of his command, and the Kaiser summoned Hindenburg, the faithful Ludendorff at his side, to take his place as Chief of the General Staff.

### The Battle of the Somme

By this time there had been a further development on the Western Front. We have seen how at the Chantilly Conference the previous November the Allied High Command had agreed that in 1916 they would combine their forces, east and west, in a common offensive. The western contribution would be an attack by the British and French armies at their point of junction east of Amiens on the river Somme. Originally the forces contributed would have been about equal, but when the attack opened in July their heavy commitment at Verdun had reduced the French share to six first-line divisions as against the British nineteen. The British did not complain. This was the test for which their New Armies had been preparing for the previous two years. Their preparations were as meticulous, far-reaching, and clearly signalled as would be those for the landings in Normandy twenty-eight years later. Their attack was preceded by a week-long artillery bombardment in which a million and a half shells were fired: 'The wire has never been so well cut,' wrote General Haig on the eve of battle, 'nor artillery preparations so thorough'. So effective did he believe them to have been that many of the 120,000 men who went 'over the top' on the morning of 1 July were not equipped for an assault at all, but burdened with equipment to fortify positions already conquered for them by the artillery.

It did not work out like that. A large percentage of the shells fired, hastily manufactured by unskilled labour, were duds. Those that did explode failed to destroy defences dug deep into the chalk hillside, from which machine-gunners emerged, when the barrage lifted, to fire point-blank at the long lines of overloaded troops plodding across the bare chalk slopes towards them. Once the battle had begun, the careful co-operation between infantry and artillery on which so much depended disintegrated in the fog of war. By the end of the day 21,000 men were dead or missing.

Had the battle ended in spectacular success, these losses, which were no worse than those suffered by the French and Russian armies during the previous two years many times over, might have been regarded as an acceptable price to pay. Instead they became, in the British group memory, the epitome of incompetent generalship and pointless sacrifice. But there was no such success. The attacks continued for a further four months. By then the Allied armies had advanced about ten miles, the Somme battlefield had been churned, like that of Verdun, into a featureless lunar landscape, and the Allies had lost a total of 600,000 men. The size of the German losses has been a matter of furious controversy, but they were probably little less than those of the Allies, and the sufferings of their troops under continuous artillery bombardment had been no less terrible. Since the object of the attack had always been unclear—Haig's own expectations of a breakthrough had never been shared by his subordinate commanders—the Allies claimed a victory in terms of attrition. Indeed by the end of the year they, like their German adversaries, could see no other way of winning the war.

### Brusilov's Offensive

Paradoxically it was the Russians, now almost written off by both sides, whose contribution to the Allied offensive of 1916 was to be one of the most successful of the entire war. In March they had attacked in the northern part of the front towards Vilna, but, in spite of having accumulated a superiority not only in men but in guns and ammunition, they had been repulsed with a loss of 100,000 men. None the less they kept their promise to their allies by launching, in June, an attack on the Galician front under General Alexei Brusilov that tore a twenty-mile gap in the Austrian armies, penetrated to a depth of sixty miles, and took half a million prisoners. Brusilov's success can be partly attributed to the low morale of the Austrian forces and the abysmal quality of their High Command, together with the apparently limitless courage of the Russian troops themselves. But yet more important were the thought and preparation that had gone into the operation: the detailed planning, the close co-operation between infantry and artillery, the immediate availability of reserves to exploit success, and, above all, the measures taken to secure surprise. It was an indication that armies were at last beginning to feel their way out of the tactical deadlock.

For the Russians it was to be a Pyrrhic victory. Their armies suffered nearly a million further casualties, and never recovered. Their success nerved their neighbour Romania, the last of the Balkan neutrals, to join the Allies, but the Rumanian army proved almost laughably incompetent, and was to be rapidly defeated in an autumn campaign by an Austro-German–Bulgarian offensive under the command of no less a figure than Falkenhayn, who was able to do something to retrieve his badly battered reputation. Rumania was overrun, together with oil and grain resources that the Central Powers were beginning so desperately to need. But it still brought the prospect of victory no nearer. The question was now being asked on both sides with increasing urgency: if there was no prospect of victory, why not make peace?

# 6

# The United States Enters the War

## Domestic Pressures at the Beginning of 1917

The original protagonists in the war, the Russian and Austrian empires, were now more than ready for peace. The pressures on their home fronts had become almost intolerable. Everywhere there were shortages of food, fuel, and raw materials for industry—the result not so much of Allied blockade as of the insatiable demands on the economy of the military sector. Raging inflation drove consumer goods onto a black market. The beneficiaries were profiteers from war industries whose boldly flaunted new wealth intensified social tensions. Peasants could still hoard their stocks and resort to a barter economy, so the worst sufferers were the working and lower-middle classes in the cities, who had to queue for hours, often in bitter cold, for such low-quality goods as were available. Strikes and bread riots became endemic throughout Central and Eastern Europe. Domestic hardships, combined with the losses suffered by their armies, left little room for the patriotic sentiment and dynastic loyalty that had sustained the Czarist and Habsburg regimes over the previous two years, and by the end of 1916 it was clear that the two empires were engaged in a race for disintegration. The death of the 86-year-old Emperor Franz-Joseph in November was widely seen to presage the end of the Empire itself. His successor, the young Emperor Karl, at once established 'back channels' with France to discuss peace terms. German influence was still strong enough both to sustain Austria's war effort and to quash her search for peace; but Czar Nicholas II's western allies could do nothing to help him when, three months later, bread riots in Petrograd spun out of control and brought down his regime.

Those western allies were not yet ready for peace. For one thing efficient and largely uncorrupt bureaucracies could manage their economies competently enough to avoid serious civilian hardship. For another, command of the seas gave them access to the foodstuffs and raw materials of the western hemisphere. The question of payment for these was to store up huge problems for the future, but for the moment credit was plentifully available. War weariness was certainly growing in both France and Britain. In both countries socialists whose pre-war international loyalties had been temporarily overlaid by patriotic fervour were now beginning to argue for a compromise peace, but they were still in a small minority, and political discontent was directed rather at the conduct of the war than at its continuance. In both countries, the increasing mobilization of civilian resources was leading to growing civilian participation in the management of the war itself. In France, the sacrifices of Verdun were blamed on the misjudgements of Joffre, who was replaced by a politically more acceptable general, Robert Nivelle. In Britain Haig's position remained unassailable in spite of the losses of the Somme, but popular discontent found its target in the somewhat lackadaisical administration of Herbert Asquith. In December Asquith was replaced as Prime Minister by David Lloyd George—a 'man of the people', one rightly credited with the creation of the civil infrastructure that supported the war effort and who had the charisma of a natural war leader. The general mood both in France and in Britain at the end of 1916 was not so much in favour of making peace—certainly not so long as the Germans remained in Belgium and north-east France—as of making war more efficiently.

This was the mood also of Germany's military leaders. Whereas in France and Britain military setbacks had led to an assertion of civilian leadership, in Germany military successes, especially on the Eastern Front, had so enhanced the reputation of Hindenburg and Ludendorff that, when they displaced Falkenhayn in command of the army in August 1916, they virtually took control of the country as well. But, although Falkenhayn had lost office, his ideas had triumphed. The experience of Verdun and the Somme persuaded his successors that the nature of the war had fundamentally changed. It was no longer a conflict to be resolved on the battlefield by superior military skill and morale, but one of endurance between industrial societies in which control of armed forces melded seamlessly into control of production and the allocation of available resources. Civilians were as intrinsic a part of war making as the military, and so logically should be under military control. The High Command therefore created a Supreme War Office, an *Oberstekriegsamt*, to control both industry and labour, and passed an Auxiliary Service Law, the *Helfdienstgesetz*, which made the entire population liable for conscription. The military in fact created a shadow bureaucracy, paralleling the civilian, and competing with it in running the country. Soldiers became bureaucrats. They also became politicians. Ludendorff's staff fomented a campaign for the triumphalist war aims first set out in the September programme of 1914—permanent control of Belgium and northern France, together with widespread annexations of territory in Poland and the *OberOst*.

By doing so they worsened the tensions that were now beginning to pull German society apart. The Social Democrats, whose voting strength lay among the urban working classes, were the strongest party in the *Reichstag*, which still had the power to vote war credits. In 1914 they had been persuaded to support what had been depicted as a defensive war against Russian aggression. Now the Russians had been soundly defeated. Working-class solidarity was disrupted by the army's intelligent policy of cooperation with the trade unions and lavish wage increases in war-related industries, but agitation was growing for a peace 'without annexations or indemnities', and found growing support in cities where food shortages were already producing bread riots. Failure of the potato crop in the autumn of 1916 forced the urban poor to subsist throughout the winter on a diet largely of turnips. The terrible losses at Verdun and the Somme—a million and a half men dead or wounded—had taken their toll of German morale, both civil and military. However successful the High Command might be in squeezing more productivity out of the German economy, it was increasingly doubtful whether the German people would support the war for another year.

8  Hindenburg and Ludendorff: masters of wartime Germany

### *Unrestricted Submarine Warfare*

It was against this background that the German government took its fatal decision to strike at the very root of its enemy's industrial strength by resorting to unrestricted submarine warfare. They understood the risk they were running, that this would probably bring the United States into the war, but calculated that by the time American participation became effective the war would have been won. It was, as a German statesman put it, Germany's last card; 'and if it is not trumps, we are lost for centuries'. He was not far wrong.

In 1914 few navies had understood the potential of the submarine. The range of the first petrol-driven models made them suitable only for coastal defence, and even when, shortly before the war, submarines were equipped with diesel-driven engines, they remained basically 'submersibles'—highly vulnerable on the surface and with a very limited submerged capacity. Their potential lethality was demonstrated within weeks of the outbreak of war when, as we have seen, a German submarine had sunk three unwary British cruisers in the Channel. But warships were regarded as fair game. Unarmed merchantmen were not. Over some three centuries of trade warfare the maritime powers of Europe had evolved elaborate rules for the treatment of merchant vessels on the high seas in wartime. Belligerents had the right to stop and search them for 'contraband',— that is, materials of war. If any was found, the vessel had to be escorted to the nearest port, where a 'prize court' would adjudicate whether the cargo was contraband or not, and confiscate it if it was. If for any reason this was not possible, the vessel might be destroyed, but only after the passengers and crew had been put in a place of safety. For a submarine, none of this was possible. They had no space either for a spare crew to man captured vessels or to accommodate their prisoners. If they surfaced to give warning of attack, they were vulnerable to any armaments their victim might be carrying, and to having their position instantly revealed by his radio; but to sink the vessel without warning and without saving her crew was, in the view of pre-war naval strategists, 'unthinkable'.

None the less, blockade had always been central to the conduct of war between maritime powers, and the advent of industrialization had made it more central than ever. In wars between agrarian societies, blockade could destroy only trade and with it the wealth that enabled states to carry on the war. Populations could still feed themselves. But blockade of industrialized societies, especially ones so highly urbanized as Britain and Germany, would not only interrupt trade and so (it was believed) create financial chaos, but destroy industries by depriving them of imported raw materials, to say nothing of starving urban populations by depriving them of imported foodstuffs. This was the nightmare that had haunted pre-war British planners and publicists when they contemplated the implications of losing 'command of the sea'; and this was the weapon by which the British Admiralty had hoped to achieve victory over Germany without the need for any major military commitment to the Continent.

By 1916 the British blockade was achieving all that had been expected of it. The Germans were able to make marginal evasions through neighbouring neutral powers— Holland, Denmark, and Scandinavia—and their scientists, as we have seen, had devised home-produced substitutes for

such essential imports as textiles, rubber, sugar, and especially nitrates for explosives and artificial fertilizer. None the
less, the pressure was becoming quite literally lethal. Mortal-
ity among women and small children had increased by 50
per cent and hunger-related diseases such as rickets, scurvy,
and tuberculosis were endemic. By the end of the war official
German estimates attributed 730,000 deaths directly to the
blockade. Probably this was an overestimate: many of the
shortages were in fact due to distortions of the economy
resulting from the enormous demands of the military. But
government propaganda could plausibly attribute all the
hardships being suffered by the civil population to British
brutality. Why should the British not be made to suffer in
their turn?

To make them do so appeared not only possible but, in the
eyes of most Germans, entirely legitimate. The British had
already stretched if not broken international law when in
November 1914 they had declared the whole of the North
Sea a 'war zone' in which neutral shipping could proceed
only if licensed by the Royal Navy. The Germans retaliated
the following February by declaring all approaches to the
British Isles a war zone in which they would seek to destroy all
hostile merchant ships, 'without being able to guarantee the
safety of the persons and goods they were carrying'. Three
months later the British further escalated the situation by
announcing their intention of seizing and confiscating any
goods they suspected of being destined for Germany, whatever their ownership or alleged destination—thus effectively
imposing a total blockade of all trade with Germany
irrespective of neutral rights and legal definitions of contraband. This aroused huge protests in the United States, which

had gone to war with Britain 100 years earlier over precisely this issue; but hardly had these got under way when, on 6 May 1915, a German U-boat sank the British luxury liner the *Lusitania* off the south coast of Ireland on a voyage from New York. The vessel was certainly carrying contraband in the shape of ammunition, and the German consulate in New York had warned American citizens that they travelled on it at their own risk. But nevertheless 128 of them did and most of them perished, together with over 1,000 fellow-passengers.

The shock to world opinion was comparable to the sinking of the *Titanic* three years earlier, and was exploited to the hilt by British propaganda as yet another example of German 'frightfulness'. It was now clear that, in the battle for American public opinion, Germany was at a major disadvantage: whereas the British blockade cost the Americans only money, the German cost them lives. After another passenger ship, the *Arabic*, was sunk the following August, even though only two US lives were lost, American protests became so violent that the German navy forbade their U-boat commanders to sink at sight, and withdrew them from the Atlantic and the Channel altogether. This meant that German U-boat commanders now had to operate according to the laws of 'cruiser warfare', which involved surfacing to identify and halt suspected vessels (which were often armed, and might even be British warships disguised as unarmed neutrals) and ensuring that passengers and crew were safely in their lifeboats before sinking their ship, thus giving time for their victims to radio their position and that of their attackers. Even so, the losses they inflicted were serious. By the end of 1915 they had sunk 885,471 tons of Allied shipping; by the end of 1916, a further 1.23 million tons. The Royal Navy seemed powerless to stop them. What might they not do if their hands were untied?

The German Naval Staff set up an expert study group to consider this question, which came up with some remarkable results. It concluded that the British had available only some eight million tons of shipping for all purposes. If the rate of sinking could be increased to 600,000 tons a month and neutral shipping were scared off, within six months Britain would run out of such essential foodstuffs as grain and meat; her coal production would be hit by lack of Scandinavian timber for pit props, which would reduce her produc-

9 President Wilson: Prophet of Peace

tion of iron and steel, and that in its turn would reduce her capacity to replace the lost shipping. British surrender within six months was thus statistically certain, whether or not the United States came into the war.

Even for many in Germany who were not privy to these calculations the case for unrestricted submarine warfare now seemed overwhelming, and a public debate was waged over the question throughout the latter half of 1916. On the one side were the navy, the High Command, and the political forces of the right. On the other were the Foreign Office, Chancellor von Bethmann Hollweg, and the Social Democrats in the *Reichstag*. Bethmann Hollweg did not trust the statistics. He was convinced that urestricted submarine warfare would bring the United States into the war, and that this would guarantee Germany's defeat. But he could see no alternative except making peace; and the only peace terms the High Command was prepared to contemplate were ones that the Allies would certainly not accept.

### The Failure of Peace Efforts

The President of the United States, Woodrow Wilson, had been urging the belligerents to make peace since the beginning of the war. American public opinion tended to favour the Allies on ideological grounds, strengthened by social links between the 'Wasp' (White Anglo-Saxon Protestant) ascendancy of the east coast and the British ruling classes. There was strong pressure led by ex-President Theodore Roosevelt for immediate intervention on the side of the democracies. Sympathy for the Central Powers was slight, and the image of Germany as a militaristic monster projected by her behaviour in Belgium, her use of poison gas, and her ruthless conduct of the war at sea, all powerfully magnified by Allied propaganda, did nothing to increase it. But the British were not generally popular either. In addition the substantial Irish vote in the cities of the east and the ethnic German communities further west, there were many who regarded Britain not as a natural ally but as the traditional enemy against whom the United States had already fought two major wars and might have to fight another if she were to establish her rightful place as a World Power. Still, the overwhelming majority of Americans favoured keeping out of a war that was none of their business. Yet as the war went on an increasing amount of that business consisted in supplying war material to the Allies—not necessarily out of ideological sympathy, but because they could not get it to the Germans. If that trade were interrupted, then the war would become their business, whether they liked it or not.

Until the end of 1916 President Woodrow Wilson's primary concern had been to keep the United States out of the war. But the longer the war went on, the more difficult this became. His problem was less to persuade the hard-pressed Allies to make peace: that could always be done by cutting off their credits and supplies, which Wilson showed himself quite ready if necessary to do. It was how to persuade the victorious Germans, who were not getting American supplies anyway. Throughout 1915 and 1916 Wilson's personal emissary, the Anglophile Colonel House, had been exploring possibilities of a settlement, but the German armies were still too successful, and the Allies too hopeful of eventual military success, for either side to consider it.

By the end of 1916 the situation was changing. In November Wilson was elected President for a second term, and, although both his personal inclination and his government's official policy were still to keep America out of the war, his hand had been strengthened against the isolationists. In Europe the pressure for peace was becoming too strong for any belligerent government to ignore. Even Ludendorff had to take account of the plight of his Austrian ally and the growing demand within the *Reichstag* for a peace 'without annexations or indemnities'. Shortly after his re-election Wilson invited the belligerents to state their peace terms. The Allies were happy to do so, knowing that these would command American sympathy. They involved, first and foremost, the restoration of Belgian and Serb independence with full indemnity for the damage done by their occupiers. In addition, they required 'the restitution of provinces or territories wrested in the past from the Allies by force'; Alsace-Lorraine, obviously, but perhaps other territories as well. Italians, Slavs, Rumanians, Czechs, and Slovaks were to be liberated from foreign domination (the fact that Italy had been promised extensive Slav territories by the Treaty of London was left unstated). Poland was to be granted independence—a concession that the Czar, under intense Allied pressure, had already accepted for the Polish territories under his control. Finally, the Ottoman Empire was to be dismembered, though on what lines was left unspecified.

The terms sought by the German High Command, on the other hand, were so extreme that Bethmann Hollweg dared not make them public for fear of their effect, not simply on the Americans but on the *Reichstag*. He confidentially communicated to Wilson a watered-down version, explaining that these were the best that he could make acceptable to his colleagues. Belgium would not be annexed outright, but her independence would depend on political, economic, and military guarantees that would make her virtually a German protectorate. Not only would Alsace and Lorraine remain in German hands, but France should also surrender the neighbouring ore-bearing land around Briey. In the east, German protectorates would be established over Poland and the Baltic provinces that would ensure their continuing Germanization. Austrian dominance should be restored in the Balkans, and colonial territories yielded in Africa. Had the Germans won the war, these were probably the best terms that the Allies could have expected. The same would have been true of the Allied terms for a defeated Germany. But neither side was yet defeated. In spite of war weariness, their governments were prepared to fight on rather than make peace on the only terms available.

To pacify the *Reichstag*, the German government issued a 'Peace Note' on 12 December. While declaring a general readiness for peace, this stated no specific war aims, and its bellicose tone made it easy for the Allies to reject it out of hand. This rejection gave the High Command the excuse it needed. The decision was taken on 9 January, but it was not until 31 January that the German Ambassador in Washington informed the American government that unrestricted submarine warfare on all vessels approaching the British Isles would commence the following day.

Wilson immediately broke off relations with Germany. He did not yet declare war. 'Armed neutrality', whereby the United States would arm and protect its own shipping, still seemed a possible alternative. But the German government assumed that war was now inevitable. On that assumption the German Foreign Minister, Arthur Zimmerman, had already on 16 January cabled the Mexican government, which was in a condition of intermittent hostilities with the United States, proposing an alliance in which they should 'make war together, make peace together, with generous financial support and an understanding on our part that Mexico is to reconquer the lost territories in Texas, New Mexico and Arizona'. The British had intercepted and decoded this remarkable document as soon as it was sent, but they did not reveal its contents to Wilson until 24 February. Natural suspicions that it might be a British forgery were laid at rest by Zimmerman himself, who frankly acknowledged its authorship.

The reaction in the United States, especially in the hitherto isolationist west, was cataclysmic. It took only a few more sinkings to convince Wilson himself that he had no alternative but to invite Congress to declare war. This he did on 5 April 1917. There was now no talk, as Wilson had suggested a few months earlier, of 'Peace without Victory'. This war would be, in his words, a crusade 'for democracy, for the right of those who submit to authority to have a voice in their own governments, for the rights and liberties of small nations, for a universal dominion of right by such a concert of free peoples as shall bring peace and safety to all nations and make the world itself free.' Admirable as these intentions were, they were very different from those with which the peoples of Europe had gone to war three years earlier.

# 7

# 1917: The Year of Crisis

## *Tactical Developments on the Western Front*

It still remained an open question whether the United States' entry into the war could save the Allies from defeat. As 1917 wore on, this seemed increasingly doubtful.

Ludendorff did not intend to waste any more German lives. He now planned to stand on the defensive in the west until the U-boat offensive had achieved its expected results. A tour of the Somme battlefields had appalled him. Falkenhayn's policy had been to hold every inch of ground regardless of cost. As a result, the sufferings of the German troops at Verdun and on the Somme had been at least comparable with those of their attackers. Given that the German front lay deep inside French territory, some elasticity in defence seemed quite justifiable. Ludendorff therefore ordered a general withdrawal from the projecting salient between Arras and Soissons, abandoning all the Somme battlefields that had been so bitterly defended, to a shorter and well-fortified 'Hindenburg line' (the British title) some twenty-five miles in the rear. In the course of this withdrawal German troops trashed or burned all habitations, slaughtered the cattle, and poisoned the wells—activities commonplace enough on the Eastern Front, but only confirming the barbaric image that Germany now presented to the west.

The new defences were laid out on new principles. No longer were troops crammed into front-line trenches to provide easy targets for enemy artillery. Trench lines were replaced by defended zones, based on widely separated machine-gun emplacements in concrete 'pillboxes' defended by barbed wire and covered by pre-ranged artillery. The bulk of the infantry was kept back out of range of the enemy guns, ready to counter-attack. Behind these forward zones lay others in sufficient depth to make any breakthrough almost impossible. Not only would such positions require fewer troops to defend them, but enemy artillery fire would fall largely on open ground and only add further obstacles to infantry attack.

The offensive riposte to such defences had already been explored on the Eastern Front the previous year with Brusilov's offensive: brief but intense artillery barrages in great depth on selected targets, followed by infantry attacks with reserves held well forward to penetrate between enemy strong points and cause confusion in rear areas. The French had also been thinking along similar lines. Their new commander-in-chief, Robert Nivelle, had had some success with them at Verdun, and was anxious to try them out on a larger scale. But what had worked against an Austro-Hungarian army already on the brink of dissolution would not necessarily work against the Germans, and the British were a great deal more cautious. They had themselves been developing caterpillar-tracked armoured vehicles, 'tanks', and had experimented with a few on the Somme; but the early models were so clumsy and mechanically defective that only their most enthusiastic protagonists expected that they could do more than help the infantry break into the enemy first line of defence. British tactical doctrine had been developing along different lines. For the British the 'queen of the battlefield' was now the artillery. By 1917 they possessed guns and ammunition that were both reliable and available in sufficient quantities. Improvements in observation, whether from aircraft or by sound ranging or flash sightings, now made possible almost pinpoint accuracy in counter-battery fire. Improvements in mapping, air photography, and meteorological analysis now enabled gunners to target objectives from map references without losing surprise by firing sighting shots. Instantaneous fuses and gas or smoke shells made possible heavy and lethal barrages that did not make ground impassable to assaulting infantry. Finally, British gunners had perfected the 'creeping barrage'—an advancing line of gunfire behind whose cover the infantry could assault to within yards of the enemy positions.

The trouble was that all this demanded the most exact timing and elaborate staff work. The infantry themselves were adjusting to meet the requirements of trench warfare, with light machine guns, hand grenades, and trench mortars supplementing if not replacing rifles as their staple armaments; but their action was still confined within a rigid framework determined by the needs and timetables of gunners with whom communications were still primitive; and, once the battle began, those communications still fell apart. Further, once the initial objectives had been attained, the guns had to be re-ranged, if not physically moved forward, to engage further targets. As a result, the British High Command had developed a technique that became known as 'bite and hold': carefully prepared attacks against limited objectives, which were then fortified and held while preparations were made for the next phase of attack. Within its limits this technique was very successful; but not only was it of little value in achieving the 'breakthrough' of which Haig himself still dreamed, but it discouraged the kind of initiative at lower levels of command that was now commonplace within the German army.

### The Allied Offensives in Spring 1917

Using such techniques as these, the Allied High Command hoped that their offensives of 1917 would not repeat the disasters of the previous year. But the losses suffered at Verdun and on the Somme had eroded the confidence that the French and British governments had hitherto placed in their military leaders. Joffre, as we have seen, had been replaced by Nivelle. Lloyd George did not quite dare do the same with Haig, but in a devious intrigue he subordinated him to French command—a manœuvre from which relations between British military and civilian leadership never recovered. Nivelle's own optimism was not shared by his fellow-generals. His political support was undermined by the overthrow of the French Premier Aristide Briand, whose successors had little confidence in Nivelle's military plans. When on 16 April Nivelle launched his much-heralded offensive across the Aisne against the wooded heights of the Chemin des Dames, it was under the worst possible auspices. The

Germans had received ample advance warning French plans had been disrupted by the German withdrawal to the Hindenburg line; and the weather was terrible. Instead of the promised breakthrough, there was a painful advance of a few miles that had to be called off after ten days, by which time the French had suffered over 130,000 casualties. Nivelle was replaced by Pétain, the hero of Verdun, but by now the French army had had enough. It collapsed, not so much into mutiny as into the equivalent of a civil strike, whole units refusing to obey orders and return to the front. Pétain gradually nursed it back to health with a minimum of severity, largely by improving its conditions and refraining from any major offensive actions, but the French army on the Western Front could make little further contribution for the remainder of the year.

The British did better—at least to begin with. A week before the opening of the French offensive across the Aisne they had attacked further east, at Arras. The first phase of the operation succeeded brilliantly, with Canadian troops seizing the dominating Vimy Ridge. Haig again hoped for a breakthrough, but the new German defences baffled him. The British offensive once more gradually slowed down until it was broken off at the end of May with a loss of a further 130,000 men. But there could be no question in Haig's mind of suspending his attacks. By this time not only the French, but also the Russians, were *hors de combat*; no effective help would be forthcoming from the United States for another year; and, worst of all, the German submarine campaign seemed to be succeeding. As a wag put it at the time, 'The question is, whether the British Army can win the war before the Navy loses it.'

## Sea and Air Warfare

At first unrestricted submarine warfare seemed likely to achieve all the results the German navy had promised. Their target had been to sink 600,000 tons of shipping a month, doubling the previous rate. They reached it in March. In April they went on to sink 869,000 tons. There they peaked. Sinkings hovered around the 600,000 ton mark all summer, were down to 500,000 tons in August, and by the end of the year had fallen to 300,000 tons. Why?

The most obvious reason was the introduction of convoys, a system that the Admiralty had declared impracticable since, among other reasons, it believed that it did not have enough destroyers to escort the amount of shipping involved. Since it included all coast-wise shipping in its calculations, it was proved badly wrong, and when, at the insistence of Lloyd George, convoys were introduced at the beginning of April, their success was immediate. Once the Americans began to make their weight felt, they were able not only to reinforce convoy protection but to build merchant vessels faster than submarines could sink them. The Germans had also miscalculated the cargo space available to the Allies, the degree of British dependence on grain imports, and above all the British capacity for counter-measures in the form of commerce control and commodity allocation through rationing. The British government indeed operated a siege economy so successfully that by the end of 1917 its grain reserves had actually doubled.

None of this, however, was apparent in the summer of 1917, when the population of London was subjected to yet another ordeal: daylight bombing from the air.

The importance of air power had not been under-estimated by any of the belligerents before 1914. For ten years previously imaginative fiction had depicted the horrors of air bombardment of cities by aircraft that had yet to be invented, but the military themselves were more concerned with the effect of aircraft on surface warfare—in particular their capacity to carry out the reconnaissance operations that could no longer be undertaken by cavalry. But, since such reconnaissance was possible only if uninterrupted by enemy aircraft, the main function of the air arm rapidly became to establish command of the air over the battlefield, whether by direct air combat or by destruction of enemy airfields. In single combat between air aces above the mud of the trenches, the traditional romance of war enjoyed a very brief revival.

'Strategic bombardment', attack on the civil resources of the enemy, was slower to develop. German dirigible balloons, named after their chief sponsor the Graf von Zeppelin, had attacked Antwerp in August 1914 (British aircraft responded against Zeppelin sheds in Düsseldorf in October) and began night raids on the United Kingdom the following January. But their navigation was too inaccurate and their destructive power too slight for these raids to be more than a dramatic nuisance; one, however, that provided propagandists with further evidence of German 'frightfulness'. By 1917 more reliable long-range aircraft had been developed, and that summer German Gotha bombers carried out daylight raids on London. The physical damage and casualties were slight but the moral effect was enormous. Against the advice of the military, who needed all the resources they could get for the war in France, an Independent Air Force was formed, based in eastern France, with the task of retaliating against German territory. Since the only targets within range were the towns of the upper Rhine the immediate impact of these operations was negligible, but in the long run their implications were far-reaching. On the very inadequate evidence of their success the newly formed Royal Air Force was to build a doctrine of strategic bombing that would dominate British and later American strategic thinking for the rest of the twentieth century.

### The Collapse of the Eastern Front

Meanwhile the Eastern Front was disintegrating. In January there was still hope that the Russian army, now well supplied with guns and ammunition, might still play its part in a joint spring offensive. But in February its commanders confessed that morale was so low, and desertion so general, that they could no longer rely on their troops. The morale of the army only reflected that of the country as a whole. Revolutionary agitation, common enough before the war but anaesthetized when hostilities began, was now almost unchecked. In March bread riots in Petrograd turned to revolution when the police and army made common cause with the rioters. The Czar was persuaded to abdicate. A regime of bourgeois moderates took over the machinery of government, but an alternative focus of power was established in the capital by a council (Soviet) of soldiers and workers, which established a network of alternative authority throughout the country and called for an immediate peace.

These events were at first welcomed in the West, not least

in the United States. Czarist Russia had been an embarrassing ally in a war fought to make the world safe for democracy, and the new government under Alexander Kerensky declared its intention of continuing the war for the defence of the Russian homeland. In July Brusilov attempted to repeat his triumph of the previous year with a major offensive on the Galician front, with some initial success. Then the Germans counter-attacked in the north. The Russian defences crumbled. Retreat became a rout, and the speed of the German advance was determined only by their ability to keep up with Russian troops now 'voting with their feet' and going home. In September the Baltic fortress of Riga fell after a hurricane bombardment devised by the innovative genius of a certain Colonel Bruchmuller. Meanwhile in Petrograd a revolutionary leader, Vladimir Ilyich Ulianov Lenin, whose views had been regarded as too extreme by all but his closest colleagues and whose return from exile in Switzerland had been sagaciously facilitated by the German High Command, had been voicing the demands of the huge majority of his countrymen in three simple words: bread, land, and peace. In November he precipitated a second *coup d'état*. This created not a vacuum of power as had that in March, but a ruthless dictatorship whose immediate aims commanded the support of the Russian people even if its programme and ideology did not. Lenin immediately asked the German High Command for an armistice, and in December both sides met to discuss peace terms at Brest-Litovsk.

## *Passchendaele*

Although disaster on so catastrophic a scale had not been foreseen by the Western allies in the summer of 1917, they had no illusions about the state of the Russian army. Indeed its weakness provided one of the strongest arguments in favour of continuing pressure on the Western Front, and against the policy, increasingly attractive to the French High Command, of remaining on the defensive and awaiting the arrival of the Americans in 1918. By then the Russians might well be out of the war and the Germans able to concentrate all their forces on breaking the Western allies. But the French were no longer calling the shots, and their collapse left the British High Command, for the first time, in a position to determine its own operational strategy.

Sir Douglas Haig, with some reason, now saw the outcome of the war as resting on his shoulders and the armies of the British Empire under his command. He had little expectation that the Americans would arrive in time, and in sufficient numbers, to prevent disaster. In his view the only hope of victory was to continue the grinding pressure on the German people through the attrition of their army. This should now be done in Flanders over the old battlefields round Ypres, where the British army could fight unencumbered by its allies and where a substantial advance might capture the Belgian ports used by the U-boats as their forward bases—an idea endorsed, naturally enough, by the Royal Navy. Such an advance, Haig believed, could be achieved by a series of limited attacks following so fast on each other that the Germans would have no time to recover. Lloyd George, dreading a repeat of the Somme holocaust, was openly sceptical about

10 The Western Front: the battlefield of Passchendaele

the plans, but after his misjudgement over the Nivelle affair he felt in no position to veto them. Indeed, a preliminary attack launched against the Messines ridge south of Ypres at the beginning of June, with limited objectives, total surprise and massive artillery support (3.5 million shells were fired and the German front line destroyed by 0.5 million kilograms of high-explosive mines) proved one of the greatest tactical successes of the war. But when the main attack opened at the end of July, it ran into all the problems that had beset the campaign on the Somme. The preliminary barrage (4.3 million shells) had forfeited all surprise; its elaborate timetables were disrupted as usual by the friction of war; enemy resistance was in greater depth and more determined than had been expected; and heavy rain assisted the guns of both sides to churn the battlefield into impassable mud. None the less, Haig battled on, achieving limited successes at huge cost, until at the beginning of November Canadian troops captured the ridge of Passchendaele, after which the entire battle came to be named. By that time the British had lost a further 240,000 men, 70,000 of them dead. German losses totalled about 200,000. Haig's critics look at the former figures; his defenders at the latter. If we consider the effect of this pressure on the German people themselves, it must be said that his defenders have a stronger case than has generally been admitted. But the price was almost unbearably heavy.

Haig's critics were provided with further ammunition when, on 20 November, he launched a second attack, at Cambrai. Part of his object was to try out on a large scale the new techniques that had been developing within the British army of close cooperation between the three arms of infantry, tanks, and artillery. Surprise was complete; German defences were overrun to a depth of four miles, and in England church bells were rung to celebrate the victory. They were premature. Ten days later the Germans counter-attacked and retook all the ground they had lost. As a result, Haig lost his last vestige of credit with his political masters, and Lloyd George took over the strategic conduct of the war.

### Caporetto

The losses on the Somme in 1916 had left Lloyd George deeply sceptical about the wisdom of continuing to attack on the Western Front at all, and throughout 1917 he had been urging the High Command to look elsewhere. Two theatres appeared more promising: Italy and the Middle East.

The Italian front had been active throughout 1916. For the Austrians, as we have seen, Italy was always the preferred adversary. In May, much against the advice of his German allies, who saw no strategic advantage in doing so, Conrad launched a major offensive through the mountains of the Trentino. After an initial success it had slowed to a halt. Admittedly Conrad could claim a major victory—the Italians lost about 286,000 men, 45,000 of them prisoners of war—but its main strategic consequence had been to reduce the resources available to the Austrians when Brusilov attacked the following month. Meanwhile the main Italian armies under General Luigi Cadorna had been assaulting the strong Austrian defences forty miles further east on the Isonzo river. They continued to do so until November in a prolonged battle of attrition on the stony plateau of the Carso, north of

Trieste, which was renewed the following spring. By August 1917 Cadorna had lost over 200,000 men on this bloodiest of battlefields, and both the Italian and the Austrian armies had reached breaking point. But Ludendorff, having disposed of the Russians, could now spare resources to help his ally, and sent seven divisions to reinforce the Austrians on the Isonzo. Using all the artillery and infantry techniques they had now perfected on the Eastern Front, the Germans smashed through the Italian defences at Caporetto on 25 October, taking 30,000 prisoners. The entire Italian front collapsed, and only re-formed two weeks later seventy miles to the rear along the Piave, with the loss of 275,000 prisoners, 2,500 guns, and vast quantities of stores. In addition, about half a million Italian deserters had melted into the landscape.

For Lloyd George the Italian collapse was providential. Haig was summarily ordered to send five divisions from the Western Front, which effectively closed down his own offensive and, together with six French divisions, restored stability in the Italian theatre. More important, Lloyd George used the opportunity of an Allied conference at Rapallo on 5 November to collaborate with the new French Prime Minister Georges Clemenceau (a man after his own heart, one who had even less time for generals) in setting up an Allied Supreme War Council, consisting of the Allied political leaders with their military advisers, to lay down military policy, to allot forces to the various theatres, and, most important, to organize and allocate military supplies. Both Haig and Pétain intensely resented this usurpation of their authority, but their power had been broken. Haig's independence was still further enfeebled by the replacement of his senior staff officers, and by the removal of his greatest ally in Whitehall, the Chief of the Imperial General Staff Sir William Robertson, in favour of Lloyd George's own protégé, General Sir Henry Wilson. In both France and Britain civilian control of strategy was now complete.

Within a month of the creation of the Supreme War Council, Lloyd George received even better news. On 11 December a British army entered Jerusalem.

### The Middle East

The Turks had proved themselves a stalwart ally for the Central Powers. Their armies consisted of tough if largely illiterate peasants, whose lack of modern equipment was balanced by their own dogged courage and the leadership of young, energetic officers advised and reinforced by German experts. Their major front was the Caucasus, where they had suffered severely—first through the repulse of their unwise attack in the winter of 1914–15, then from a Russian offensive under the skilful leadership of General Nikolai Yudenich in the summer of 1916. It was in the course of that campaign that the Turkish government implemented a programme of mass deportations and massacres of the indigenous Armenian population so savage as to verge on genocide.

Simultaneously British Empire troops had invaded Turkish territory—not only from Egypt, but from the base they had established in November 1914 at Basra, at the head of the Persian Gulf, to secure the oil installations and to encourage local revolt. From there in 1915 they had advanced up the Tigris and Euphrates valleys, initially to safeguard their base but eventually in the hope of seizing Baghdad. Administratively the expedition was a disaster, its largely Indian units suffering huge casualties from sickness. It became a military catastrophe in April 1916 when, after a siege lasting nearly five months, a British force was compelled to surrender at Kut-el-Amara, some eighty miles short of Baghdad. Of the 10,000 prisoners taken, 4,000 died in captivity—a fate not shared by their commander, Major-General Charles Townsend, who enjoyed a level of hospitality at the hands of his captors that awoke very unfavourable comment. A stronger expedition was then mounted in December, which recaptured Kut and the following March occupied Baghdad.

Egypt was a British *place d'armes* second only to the United Kingdom in importance, defending as it did the line of imperial communications through the Suez Canal. After the repulse at the Dardanelles the garrison successfully defended the canal against a wildly ambitious Turkish raid across the Sinai desert in July 1916. The British then themselves advanced through the desert to the border of Palestine—an achievement made possible only by the kind of meticulous logistical planning that was to become the hallmark of British military operations in both world wars. After several attempts to break the Turkish lines at Gaza had failed in March 1917, a new British commander was sent out in the person of General Sir Edmund Allenby. Allenby had commanded an army on the Western Front without conspicuous success, but he proved himself a master of the kind of mobile warfare that was still feasible in Palestine, using mounted units in a way impossible on the Western Front together with aircraft working in close cooperation with the ground forces. Allenby's German opponent was none other than Erich von Falkenhayn, now exiled by his enemies far from the centre of power; but with all his skill Falkenhayn could do little with forces now far inferior in numbers and equipment to the British. At the end of October Allenby took the offensive, swept the Turks out of Gaza, and pressed forward to Jerusalem to provide the British people, as Lloyd George had requested, with a 'Christmas present'—one that was all the more welcome after the four-month horror of the Passchendaele campaign.

The following September—1918—Allenby was to complete the conquest of Palestine by the sweeping victory of Megiddo—a battle in which, for the last time in Western military history, mounted troops played a leading role. Pressing north, his troops had overrun Syria by the end of October, and the Turks sued for an armistice. In his advance up the coast Allenby's land flank was protected, and Turkish rail communications sabotaged, by friendly Arab forces recruited and led by the young archaeologist Colonel T. E. Lawrence. Lawrence's exploits were a marginal part of a marginal campaign, but they were to gain him a reputation that shone all the more brightly against the dismal background of the Western Front.

Allenby's victories were to establish a brief British hegemony in the Middle East. Among other things they made it possible to implement the promise made in October 1917 by the British Foreign Secretary, Arthur Balfour, to establish 'a National Home for the Jewish People' in Palestine. Unfortunately the promise was made without consulting either the indigenous population or any of the Arab potentates who had been promised the territory in return for their military support. Neither had they been consulted about an understanding reached in 1916 by British Foreign Office officials with their French opposite numbers ('the Sykes–Picot Agreement') to divide the region between their two spheres of influence. The attempt to reconcile all these irreconcilable obligations was to keep British officials busy, and the region in turmoil, until the Second World War, and created agonizing problems that at the beginning of the twenty-first century still remain unsolved.

# 8

# 1918: The Year of Decision

## *Allied Fears in January 1918*

Allenby's victories were all very well, but at the end of 1917 the prospects for the Allies still looked grim. On the credit side, the submarine war had been won, and American supplies were able to cross the Atlantic almost uninterrupted. But the Allies needed not only supplies but, yet more urgently, men, and these the Americans were slow to provide. When the United States had entered the war in April, their army consisted of 6,000 officers and 100,000 men. General John J. Pershing received orders to take the First US Division to France, but even that unit existed only on paper. Plans were made to expand the army to twenty-four divisions, about a million men, by the summer of 1918, but it seemed doubtful whether the Allies could survive so long. If they could, their worries would be over. By 1919 their superiority in both men and materiel would be enormous, and Allied staff officers began to plan a great offensive for that year. But meanwhile the nightmare that had haunted them for the past three years had come true. Russia had been knocked out of the war, leaving

*[handwritten margin note: USA / APRIL / 1918]*

Ludendorff free to concentrate all his resources against the Western Front.

Russia's defeat also had alarming implications for the British Empire. Turkey no longer had to defend her Caucasian frontiers. She had been driven out of the Arabian peninsula, but that only left her free to expand eastwards and establish a Pan-Turanian hegemony extending to the frontiers of India—a hegemony stiffened by German military muscle and inspired by a *jihad* that could undermine Britain's already precarious hold on the Indian subcontinent. It is not surprising that the American military representative on the Allied Supreme War Council should have written home in February 1918: 'I doubt if I could make anyone not present at the recent meeting . . . realize the anxiety and fear that pervade the minds of political and military men here'.

### German Fears in January 1918

But if the Allies were apprehensive, the Germans were desperate. The Russians were certainly out of the war. At Brest-Litovsk their representative Leon Trotsky had at first refused to accept terms that involved the complete abandonment of their Baltic and Polish lands to German or Austrian control; but he also refused to make peace, hoping that revolution would break out in Berlin and Vienna in time to make it unnecessary. Those revolutions were indeed to come, but not just yet. So the German armies simply advanced unopposed, not only into Finland and western Russia, but deep into the Ukraine as far as the Caucasus and the Crimea. When Lenin finally yielded in March 1918, it was on terms that involved surrendering territory containing about 90 per cent of Russia's coal resources, 50 per cent of her heavy industry, and 30 per cent of her population, as well as a payment of six billion marks in 'reparations'. In May Germany tidied up her eastern conquests by the Treaty of Bucharest, whereby Romania yielded up control of her oil production and grain surpluses and accepted an indefinite military occupation. Whatever happened in the west, the Germans had now acquired a vast, self-sufficient, and apparently impregnable eastern empire.

But it was not so much any threat from the west that now worried the German High Command. Even more alarming were developments within Germany itself.

By 1917, as we have seen, the army had taken control of the German economy. But it still did not control the *Reichstag*, and the *Reichstag* held the purse strings with its power to vote or withhold war credits—the funds without which the war could not be carried on at all. For three years patriotism had held the *Reichstag*, and indeed the whole country, together, except for a small minority of socialist dissidents. But by the winter of 1917 this unity was wearing very thin. It had been precariously preserved during the first half of that year by hope of success in the submarine offensive, but by late summer it was clear that no success was to be expected. The nation had endured four war winters, and the prospect of a fifth seemed unendurable. Scuffles in bread queues were escalating into riots, and riots into major strikes. In August 1917 the crews of naval vessels at Wilhelmshaven, bored as well as hungry, broke out in open mutiny. In January 1918 major and prolonged strikes erupted in Kiel and Berlin, and martial law had to be declared in Hamburg

**11** The pressure on the civilian population: food queue in Berlin, winter 1917

and Brandenburg. The Russian example was proving seriously infectious, and economic hardship gave edge to the swelling demand for peace.

This demand was fuelled not only by hardship but by political ideology. The despotic Czarist Empire that German liberals and socialists had always regarded as their natural enemy had been destroyed, and the new social-democratic regime in Russia seemed their natural allies. The advent of the United States had completed the unity of democratic powers against a Germany whose hegemonial ambitions as well as brutal conduct of the war German liberals and socialists were finding it increasingly hard to defend. At an International Socialist Conference in Stockholm in June 1917 the German delegates were made aware of their isolation and unpopularity. Largely in consequence of that experience, the *Reichstag* passed a Peace Resolution on 19 July by 212 votes to 126, demanding 'a peace of understanding and the permanent reconciliation of peoples without forcible acquisition of territory and without political, economic or financial measures of coercion'. Simultaneously it was voicing demands for major reforms in the archaic electoral system of Prussia and, worst of all, for the armed forces themselves to be placed under its own control.

The High Command had relied on the Chancellor, Bethmann Hollweg, to keep the *Reichstag* in order. Now that he had failed, they compelled the Kaiser to demand his resignation. His successor, a malleable bureaucrat, Georg Michaelis, agreed to accept the Peace Resolution 'as I understand it', so the war credits were passed. But clearly more would be needed to counter the peace propaganda of the left. In September the High Command sponsored the launching of a new 'Fatherland Party' to campaign against constitutional reform and support an annexationist peace. The terms of the latter were laid down in the Kreuznach Programme of 9 August. In the east, Germany would annex outright all the lands already occupied by her armies—Courland, Lithuania, and the eastern provinces of Poland. In the west she would retain Belgium and Luxembourg and gain the French regions of Longwy and Briey. The object, as Hindenburg and Ludendorff explained to the Kaiser, was 'such a strengthening of the German people, and such an improvement in our frontiers, that our enemies would not dare to let loose another war for a long time to come'. The Fatherland Party was lavishly financed by Rhine-land industrialists, but it was no mere front for the ruling classes. Within a year it numbered 1.25 million members— arguably the first genuinely populist right-wing movement of the twentieth century, and a harbinger of more to come.

The nature of the peace would thus determine not only Germany's position in Europe, but what kind of country she was going to be. In the eyes of the High Command and its civilian followers, to yield to the demands of the *Reichstag* for a peace without annexations or indemnities would be effect-ively to have lost the war—a war no longer simply against Germany's external enemies, but against all the internal forces apparently bent on destroying traditional German values. In Ludendorff's view, the only way in which those forces could be overcome before the Home Front collapsed altogether—and the even more desperate Austrians defected—was by victory on the Western Front, gained by a blow so overwhelming that the Allies would lose heart and be forced to accept the German plans for peace. This would truly be Germany's 'last card'.

### *The Ludendorff Offensive, March 1918*

Ludendorff had begun planning for that victory in Novem-ber 1917. On paper he now had more than enough troops to smash through the Western Front, as the Allies knew very well. The need to maintain order among the chaotic conditions of her vast new conquests still pinned down the great bulk of German forces in the east, but he was able to transfer some forty-four divisions to the west, bringing his total there by March 1918 to 199 divisions. Against these the French could field about 100, some of very doubtful quality, and the British fifty-eight, whose strength, as the military authorities later complained, was still further reduced by Lloyd George's policy of keeping their first-line reserves in the United Kingdom so that Haig could not use them for any further offensives. As yet the Americans could provide none at all.

The first blow was struck against the British—first an initial thrust against the southern part of their line east of Amiens, to draw in their reserves from the north, where a second blow would break through, so it was hoped, to the Channel ports. Haig, judging his left wing to be the decisive front, had deliberately weakened his right; so when the Germans attacked there on 21 March, it was with a crushing numerical superiority, some fifty-two divisions against twenty-six. But it was not numbers alone that mattered. The Germans now employed techniques that finally put an end to the deadlock of trench warfare that had immobilized the Western Front for the past three years.

The techniques were not new. A brief but violent artillery bombardment in depth without previous registration, directed as much against communications and command centres as against front-line troops and making plentiful use of gas and smoke, had already been used both by the British at Cambrai and by the Germans themselves at Caporetto. But it had been perfected on the Eastern Front, especially in the assault on Riga, by General Oskar von Hutier and his artillery commander Colonel Georg Bruchmuller, who now led the German attack in the west. The weight of their bombardment was now unprecedented: 6,500 guns fired on a forty-mile front, destroying all communications behind the lines and drenching the front line with gas and high explosive. Then 'storm troops', specialized assault-units carrying their own firepower in the shape of sled-borne light guns, light machine guns, grenades, mortars and flame-throwers, spearheaded the main infantry attack, destroying enemy strong points wherever possible and masking them when it was not. The infantry units that followed poured into the gaps they had opened, reserves being fed in to exploit success in what a British commentator, Liddell Hart, was later to describe as an 'expanding torrent'. The combination proved devastating against British troops who had barely begun to prepare the deep defences needed to counter it, or indeed to appreciate the need for them. A thick fog on the morning of 21 March assisted the German breakthrough. Within four days they had driven a wedge forty miles deep into the British positions and threatened to break the Allied lines altogether.

The attack was far more successful than Ludendorff himself had expected. It now threatened to separate the British from the French armies. If that happened, the British would have to fall back to the north along their lines of communication to the Channel ports, while the French would withdraw to the south to cover Paris, leaving the way clear for the Germans to advance to the coast—as indeed they did twenty-two years later. All now depended on the French and British armies maintaining contact. So far both Haig and Pétain had resisted the attempts of the Supreme War Council to impose an inter-allied command over their heads, and refused to place any reserves at the council's disposal to enable it to influence the course of operations. Mutual cooperation, they argued, would solve any problems that might arise. But it did not. When Haig appealed for help, Pétain refused to provide it, for fear of uncovering Paris. Haig swallowed his pride and appealed to his political superiors. An inter-allied conference met at Doullens, near Amiens, on 26 March. There the resolute stand taken by Foch, now the French Chief of Staff, impressed Haig sufficiently for him to accept Foch's authority to 'coordinate' the Allied armies—an authority extended a week later to 'the direction of operations'. For the rest of the war the Allies were to fight under a single overall command.

Meanwhile the German advance was slowing to a halt. Their communications were overextended; artillery could not keep up with the pace of the infantry advance, and progress was made more difficult by the wastelands of the Somme battlefields over which the infantry now had to advance. Captured Allied dumps certainly provided supplies in enormous quantities, but it was only too tempting for the exhausted and hungry German troops to pause and enjoy them. Ludendorff broke off the operation on 5 April and switched to the attack in the north, as Haig had been expecting. This was launched on 9 April, after the usual Bruchmuller bombardment, in the Lys valley south of the Ypres salient. Within a few days the Germans had recaptured all the ground west of Ypres that the British had taken three months and 400,000 men to conquer the previous autumn. British troops were now so thinly stretched that the usually inarticulate Haig thought it necessary to issue a dramatic

Order of the Day: 'With our backs to the wall, and believing in the justice of our cause, each one must fight on till the end. The safety of our homes and the freedom of mankind alike depend upon the conduct of each one of us at this critical moment.' This went down well with the press, though its reception by the troops themselves was more ribald. But fight on they did. The line held, and on 30 April Ludendorff broke off the attack. Since 21 March he had already lost some 350,000 men, the Allies only slightly fewer; but it was the Allies who had the longer purse, and, with American troops pouring into France at a rate of 300,000 a month, the purse was now virtually bottomless.

Ludendorff now turned on the French. The sector he chose for his attack was the Aisne, where Nivelle had launched his disastrous offensive a year earlier. On 27 May the Germans used their now familiar techniques—Bruchmuller's guns fired two million shells in four and a half hours—to crush the French Sixteenth Army, whose commanders still disdained defence in depth in favour of defending every inch of their territory. They took 50,000 prisoners and penetrated thirty miles to seize Soissons. Their long-range artillery began to bombard Paris itself, where the government once more prepared, as they had in September 1914, to move to Bordeaux. But in the course of their attack the Germans themselves lost another 130,000 men; and, most important of all, some of them had been killed by Americans.

## *The Americans Enter the Line*

Ludendorff has been criticized as much by his own country-men as by his enemies for his failure to designate any major objective for his offensive and stick to it. But, even if he had captured the Channel ports, the war would still have gone on, as it did in 1940. Even if he had taken Paris, the Americans and the British would have continued to fight. Ludendorff's object, not unlike that of Falkenhayn two years earlier, was not so much to destroy the Allied armies as to destroy the will of the Allied governments to persevere with the war and compel them to accept a compromise peace. He might have succeeded with the French. In another year it might even have been possible with the British. But it was out of the question with the United States.

By the beginning of 1918 there were already a million American troops in France, although they were not yet organized in fighting formations. From the beginning Pershing insisted that they should operate as a distinct army. He had been allotted his own front on the far right of the Allied line, in the as yet inactive theatre of Lorraine. But, although the United States could mobilize men with astonishing speed—conscription was introduced in May 1917—it took longer to tool up her industries to provide heavy weapons. Until the end of the war her army was dependent on her European allies for tanks, aircraft, and—most important of all—artillery guns and ammunition. This being so, and given the American lack of combat experience, it seemed logical to the French and British that these raw American units should, at least initially, be amalgamated with their own more experienced forces to learn their trade. This Pershing, under

President Wilson's direction, understandably refused. He did, however, allow US divisions once they were formed to serve under French command. The First Division was blooded at Cantigny on 28 May—a notable date in American military history—and two more were available to help seal the French line at Château-Thierry when the German attack penetrated thus far at the beginning of June. The gallantry of inexperience made their losses heavy—over 10,000 killed or wounded—but they learned fast; and the very presence of these tall, cheerful, well-fed boys from the Middle West with their boundless optimism convinced their weary allies that the war could not now be lost. More important, it convinced their yet more weary adversaries that it could not now be won.

Ludendorff planned a final blow against the British in the north, but after a month of indecision he decided first to launch one more violent and, he hoped, final blow against the French—a *Friedenssturm* he termed it for the benefit of his exhausted troops, a blow for peace. The blow was struck on 16 July at Reims, on the eastern edge of the salient that the Germans had now driven as far south as the Marne. But this time the French were ready for it. German deserters—their very number an indicator of German demoralization—had given warning of the attack, and the French were able to pre-empt the German bombardment with a barrage of their own. They had also at last learned the lesson of flexible defence. They allowed the Germans to bombard and occupy a front line that was empty except for barbed wire, mines, and a few machine-gun posts, before decimating them with a counter-barrage and fire from the flanks. Two days later the fiery General Mangin launched a counter-attack against the

**12** Marshal Foch and General Pershing: the New World to the rescue of the old

western flank of the salient with an army that now included American divisions. By 5 August a combined French, American, and British force had reconquered the entire salient and taken 30,000 prisoners. Ludendorff cancelled his orders for a final attack he was planning in the north. He had finally shot his bolt.

## *The Allied Counter-Attack, July 1918*

It was now the Allies' turn to take the offensive, and on 26 July Foch gave orders for a general advance on all fronts. Foch was no great strategist, but he embodied the Napoleonic maxim that in war moral forces are to physical as three to one. His infectious enthusiasm had done much to check the German advance at the Battle of the Marne in 1914. Since then his determination to attack under all circumstances had often been disastrous, but now the Allied armies had the numbers and, more important, the skills to make it effective. Pershing now had forty-two US divisions at his disposal, each twice the size of its European counterpart, and was able to regroup them in a single army—later divided into two—on the right of the Allied line. By attacking northwards through the Argonne forest, he threatened the main lateral railway line, from Metz to Antwerp, that fed the German armies. On the left of the line the British were to launch a converging attack, while French armies, reinvigorated by two fighting generals Mangin and Gouraud, kept up the pressure in the centre. Since it would take some time for the Americans to redeploy and the French to recover from the great battles of June and July, it fell to the British to launch the first blow, to the east of Amiens, on 8 August.

Considering the half a million or so losses that it had suffered since the beginning of the year, the British army had made a remarkable recovery, and of no one was this more true than Haig himself. Haig's offensive spirit, like that of Foch, had more often than not had disastrous consequences, but now, like that of Foch, its time had come. His frequent prophesies of the imminence of German collapse were at last coming true, and, unlike the majority of his colleagues who were planning a campaign for 1919, he believed that the war could be won by the end of the year. He cheerfully accepted Foch's direction from above, and, guided by his renovated staff, listened and gave effect to the new tactical concepts being developed from below. His Australian and Canadian units had proved themselves the most formidable fighters on the Western Front, and, after much trial and error, the British army had learned how to use its tanks. A successful small-scale action at Hamel on 4 July had proved a model of infantry–tank cooperation, and the same methods were now put to use on a very much larger scale. Combined with the infantry–artillery liaison techniques that the British had now mastered, and yet another innovation, the use of low-flying attack aircraft, these provided a winning combination unimaginable—and impracticable—two years earlier. Together with the French army on their right flank, the British penetrated seven miles on the first day of their attack and took 30,000 prisoners. It was the first outright and irreversible defeat that the Germans had suffered in four years of fighting, and Ludendorff himself was gloomily to describe it as 'the Black Day' of the German army.

The Germans now began a fighting retreat to the Hindenburg line established at the beginning of 1917. Their morale was still far from broken: by the time they reached the Hindenburg line early in September they had inflicted on the British a further 190,000 and on the French 100,000 losses, and the British Cabinet was again becoming anxious. None the less on 3 September Foch gave orders for a new offensive all along the line: *tout le monde à la bataille!* Pershing insisted on first blooding his new army by a limited offensive to pinch out a salient at St Mihiel in the quiet Lorraine sector, a two-day battle that was completed by 14 September, and then turned north to join in the general offensive on 26 September. The following day British and French forces assaulted the main Hindenburg line, firing a barrage of nearly a million shells in twenty-four hours. This finally broke Ludendorff's spirit. On 29 September he informed the Kaiser that there was now no prospect of winning the war. If catastrophe was to be averted, an armistice must be concluded as quickly as possible.

### The Collapse of the Central Powers

Since the beginning of August the German army had lost a further 228,000 men, half of them through desertion. Their General Staff considered fewer than fifty divisions fit for combat. Base troops, infected by increasingly gloomy news from home and vulnerable to communist propaganda, trembled on the verge of strikes, if not mutiny. But even worse was the condition of Austria-Hungary, whose emperor's desperate overtures to the French for peace terms had been cynically publicized by Clemenceau in April 1918. Their army—hungry, ragged, increasingly disintegrating into its separate ethnic elements—had been pushed into a final offensive on the Italian front on 15 June, only to be repulsed with the loss of 143,000 men, 25,000 of them prisoners. After that, the troops began to desert *en masse*. Those that remained were sick and starving, as were the populations of Vienna and other cities of the Monarchy. On 16 September the Emperor publicly appealed to President Wilson for peace terms, and tried to pre-empt ethnic disintegration by declaring the Habsburg Empire to be a federal state. When on 24 October the Italian army, powerfully reinforced by French and British divisions, at last took the offensive, the Austrian forces disintegrated after forty-eight hours, and the Allied advance could hardly keep up with the speed of their retreat. The Italians just had time to launch a last independent attack at Vittorio Veneto and reap another huge harvest of prisoners before an armistice negotiated two days earlier came into effect on 4 October.

Meanwhile the long-dormant Macedonian Front had been galvanized by the appearance of a dynamic new commander, General Franchet d'Esperey. On 15 September French and Serbian mountain troops successfully attacked hitherto impregnable Bulgarian positions. Greek and British forces joined in, and the Bulgarians, deprived of German and Austrian support, capitulated on 30 September—the first of the Central Powers to do so. The Turks followed a month later on 30 October, thus freeing themselves to continue their campaign in the Caucasus until 1919.

In Germany, six weeks were to pass before Ludendorff's decision to ask for an armistice had any result. In his eyes an armistice meant just that—a suspension of operations in the field to make possible a regrouping of his forces and negotiations leading to an agreed peace. It should be made clear, he insisted, 'that there is an unyielding determination to continue the war if the enemy will grant us no peace or only a dishonourable one.' He at last accepted that Germany would have to surrender Belgium and even Alsace-Lorraine, but he still hoped that the Allies would allow her to retain her conquests in the east as a bulwark against 'Bolshevism'. Further,

he recognized that the Allies had virtually pledged themselves not to deal with the existing regime in Berlin, so a new
one had to be installed that would bear the responsibility—
and the odium—of negotiating peace terms. So on 3 October the Kaiser appointed as Chancellor Prince Max of Baden,
a sensible moderate whom the former American Ambassador
in Berlin had described as 'one of the few high Germans who
seems to be able to think like a human being', and ordered
him to approach President Wilson with a request for an
immediate armistice. When Max demurred, the Kaiser
brusquely informed him that 'the High Command thinks it
necessary, and you have not been brought here to create
difficulties for the High Command'. Obediently the following day Max invited President Wilson, the most
approachable—or the least unapproachable—of Germany's
enemies, to take steps for the restoration of peace 'on the
basis of the moderate programme he had set forth on 8 January '—the Fourteen Points (see Appendix I).

But the Wilson of October was no longer the Wilson of
January. Then he could still see himself, and be seen, as a
figure above the battle. He had consulted no one over the
Fourteen Points—certainly not the co-belligerents he still did
not regard as 'allies'. (Since there was no formal alliance, the
United States referred to its co-belligerents simply as 'associated powers'.) But since their promulgation the Germans
had shown their own idea of peace terms with the imposition
on the Russians of the Treaty of Brest-Litovsk. More important, the United States had for the previous eight months
been involved in a shooting war in France in which a large
number of American boys had been killed. Then on 12
October a U-boat sank a passenger ship, the *Leinster*, with a

loss of several hundred British and American lives. The American people were now gripped by a war psychosis even more ferocious than that of their weary European partners. In an exchange of notes with Berlin, Wilson made it clear that he was no longer a benevolent *deus ex machina*, but the leader of a victorious and implacable alliance. He declared that 'the only armistice he would feel justified in submitting for consideration would be one which should leave the United States and the powers associated with her [*sic*] in a position to enforce any arrangements that may be entered into and make a renewal of hostilities on the part of Germany impossible'. Further, he demanded as a condition for negotiation that Germany should transform herself into a constitutional state, thus ensuring 'the destruction of every arbitrary power anywhere that can separately, secretly and of its single choice disturb the peace of the world; or if it cannot be presently destroyed, at least its reduction to virtual impotency'.

When Ludendorff learned of these conditions, he tried to break off negotiations, but his own generals would not let him. 'The morale of the troops has suffered seriously,' reported one of his army commanders, Prince Rupprecht of Bavaria, 'and their power of resistance diminishes daily. They surrender in hordes whenever the enemy attacks, and thousands of plunderers infest the districts round the bases ... Whatever happens we must make peace, before the enemy break through into Germany.' The government in Berlin had a yet more immediate fear—that of revolution breaking out in Germany itself. Max of Baden did his best to pre-empt this by cramming through in three weeks all the constitutional reforms that the Kaiser and the army had resisted for the previous half century. By the end of October the *Reichstag* found itself a sovereign body, elected on universal suffrage by secret ballot, with all government ministers responsible to it, including the Minister for War. Wilhelm II, the All Highest War Lord, found himself reduced to the status of a constitutional monarch as impotent as his cousin in England. Thus emboldened, Max now demanded the dismissal of Ludendorff, to which the Kaiser agreed with ill-concealed satisfaction. Hindenburg remained as an irreplaceable figurehead, but Ludendorff's place was taken by the equally plebeian General Wilhelm Groener, who as head of the *Oberstekriegsamt* was very familiar with the social and economic problems of the home front.

But it was all too late. The German people had suffered increasing and lately almost intolerable hardships in the belief that their armies had been, and continued to be, everywhere victorious. With the revelation that they were on the brink of collapse, all confidence in the regime disappeared. On 29 October naval crews mutinied rather than take out their ships in a 'Death-Ride' planned by their admirals to save the honour of the navy. Within a week the mutiny had spread to revolution in every big city in Germany. Workers and Soldiers' Councils seized power on the model of the Russian Soviets. Bavaria declared herself an independent republic. The rear echelons of the army mutinied and seized the crossings over the Rhine. There was wild talk at army headquarters about marching the army home and 'restoring order', but Groener knew very well that the instrument would break in his hands. He realized that revolution was inevitable unless three conditions were fulfilled. The Kaiser must abdicate; the army must support the majority party in the *Reichstag*, the Social Democrats, the only people capable of riding the political storm; and peace must be made at once, at whatever cost.

So on 9 November Groener informed the Kaiser that he no longer commanded the confidence of the army and packed him off to exile in Holland. In Berlin the leaders of the Social Democrats, Philipp Scheidemann and Friedrich Ebert, proclaimed the Republic and received assurance of army support against any incipient revolution; and a delegation was cobbled together to meet the Allied war leaders in a railway carriage in the forest near Compiègne to ask for their terms.

These terms, so far as land operations were concerned, were dictated largely by the French. The British, themselves anxious to end hostilities as quickly as possible, would have made them milder. Pershing, with two barely blooded armies straining at the leash and public opinion at home baying for 'unconditional surrender', would have granted none at all. All Belgian and French territory was to be evacuated within fourteen days; the Allies were to occupy all German territory on the Left Bank of the Rhine and a ten-kilometre belt on the Right Bank, together with bridgeheads at Mainz, Coblenz, and Cologne. All the territory conquered in Eastern Europe since 1914 was to be surrendered; massive quantities of war materiel was to be handed over, including most of the fleet and all submarines; and the Allied blockade would continue until the final signature of peace. The German delegates protested that the result would be anarchy and famine from which only the Bolshevists would profit, but Foch as leader of the Allied delegation was implacable. The Germans had no alternative but to sign what with some reason they expected to be their own death warrants. In the case of one delegate, Mathias Erzberger, it was. He was hunted down by right-wing extremists and assassinated two years later.

So on 11 November at 11 a.m., the eleventh hour of the eleventh day of the eleventh month, the guns on the Western Front at last fell silent, leaving both sides to mourn their dead.

# 9

# The Settlement

The Allied statesmen who came together in Paris in January 1919 to make the peace settlement were in a very different situation from their predecessors at Vienna in 1814. They did not have a free hand to reshape the world in conformity with the principles of order and justice, or of national self-determination, or even of the traditional balance of power. They were responsible to electorates still in the grip of war fever whose passions and prejudices could not be ignored. In any case, the mounting chaos in Central Europe in the wake of the collapse of the Russian, Austrian, and Hohenzollern empires made it doubtful whether any stable regime existed west of the Rhine with which peace could be made at all.

### *Germany*

The conference itself revolved around a tacit duel between President Wilson, who perhaps unwisely attended in person, and the French premier Georges Clemenceau. Each had a different agenda. That of Wilson was to create a new world order under the auspices of a League of Nations, to the creation of which he devoted his best endeavours; only to see his work destroyed when the United States Congress refused to participate in the League on the terms he demanded. That of Clemenceau, with the whole-hearted support of his countrymen and initially his British allies, was so to reconstruct Europe that Germany could never threaten her stability again. As we have seen, France with her population of now barely forty million faced a Germany sixty-five million-strong with a far greater industrial power and potential than France could ever command. The counterweight on which France had relied before 1914, the Russian Empire, had vanished, taking billions of francs' worth of investment with it. In the French view, therefore, everything possible had to be done to weaken Germany. In the east the maximum territory should be taken from her to build up new nations in a *cordon sanitaire* under French influence, both to ward off the encroachments of Bolshevism from the east and to take Russia's place as an instrument for the containment of German power. In the west, not only should Alsace and Lorraine with their valuable ores be restored to France, but the coal-rich Saar basin should be added to them. Further the Rhineland, the German territories on the left bank of the river, should if possible be detached from Germany altogether to constitute an autonomous state or group of states under French protection as a glacis to cover the French frontier. This the British would not accept, arguing that such a protectorate would be simply an Alsace-Lorraine in reverse, a cause of constant friction. They agreed only to the demilitarization of the left bank of the Rhine and of the right bank to a depth of forty miles, with an Allied military presence remaining pending the full payment of reparations. Ownership of the Saar coalfields was to pass to France, but the territory was to be administered by the League of Nations for fifteen years, when its destiny would be settled by plebiscite. It was a reasonable settlement, to be confirmed by the Locarno Agreement of 1924, and one not in itself likely to provoke another war.

Germany's eastern frontiers presented a far more difficult problem. One of Wilson's fourteen points had stipulated the restoration of independence to Poland, which had since the end of the eighteenth century been partitioned between Germany, Russia, and the Austrian Empire. The core of the new Poland was the Grand Duchy of Warsaw, ethnically predominantly Polish, but recognized as part of the Russian Empire since 1814. The Russians were now in no better position to contest its independence, or that of their former Baltic provinces Finland, Estonia, Latvia, and Lithuania, than were the Austrians to retain their Polish lands in Galicia. But the Polish provinces of Germany—Silesia, Posen, and West Prussia—were another matter. They had been thickly settled by Germans for generations. Worse, the new Poland had been promised access to the sea, which could be provided only by making over to her the lower Vistula valley, whose population was mixed, and the port of Danzig, which was almost entirely German. That involved dividing Germany from East Prussia, which was widely regarded as her historic heartland. The settlement was probably the best that could be achieved without the massive 'ethnic cleansing' that would take place in 1945, but the Germans never concealed their intention of reversing it at the earliest opportunity.

In addition to accepting these losses of territory, Germany was required to disarm, to surrender her overseas colonies, and to pay heavy reparations to her victorious enemies. Her army was reduced to 100,000 men and deprived of 'offensive weapons' such as tanks. Her General Staff, demonized by Allied propaganda, was disbanded; her air force was abolished; her naval building was confined to vessels of less than 100,000 tons displacement. This, so the victors argued, would 'render possible the initiation of a general limitation of the armaments of all nations'. It did not, and its failure to do so was to be used by the Germans when they denounced those restrictions and began rearming fifteen years later.

Germany lost her colonies as a matter of course, but, since the Allies under Wilson's leadership had renounced 'annexations', the powers that acquired them (mainly Britain and her overseas dominions) did so as 'mandates' on behalf of the League of Nations. The Allies had likewise renounced the 'indemnities' that defeated powers normally had to pay to their conquerors. Instead they demanded 'reparation' for the damage inflicted on their civilian populations. Initially this definition had been intended to apply to the populations of the occupied and devastated areas of France and Belgium, but the French and British rapidly extended it to cover not only such marginal expenses as interest charges on war loans and general costs of reconstruction, but pensions to disabled soldiers and to the orphans and widows of the dead in perpetuity—a sum so huge that it could not even be computed. The peace conference referred the whole matter to a Reparations Commission that was to report in 1921. Meanwhile the Germans had to pledge themselves in advance to accept the Commission's findings, and to make a down payment of twenty million marks. The Allies would keep their military forces on the Rhine to enforce payment and have the right to reoccupy German territory in the event of default.

The full implications of these demands were to be brilliantly denounced by Maynard Keynes in his philippic *The Economic Consequences of the Peace*. Eventually they were to be fudged; but not before the Germans were able to lay on them the blame for all the economic disasters that were to overwhelm them. But even more unacceptable was the justification given for imposing reparations at all—the alleged German responsibility for causing the war in the first place. The Germans still believed almost without exception that the war had been imposed on them by their enemies, and that all their sacrifices over the previous five years had been in a noble cause. Further, many felt that they had not been defeated at all. They had, it was argued, been deprived of the victory that was their due only because they had been cheated by the Allies over the Armistice terms and 'stabbed in the back' by *Reichsfeinde*, socialists and Jews, who had exploited the difficulties of the moment in order to seize power. Even for those who did not accept this myth of a *Dolchstoss* (stab in the back), the continuing legitimacy of any German government would depend on its capacity to modify the servitudes imposed by the treaty, if not abrogate them altogether. It was to be Adolf Hitler's success in doing this that was to win him such widespread support.

### Austria-Hungary

The dissolution of the Habsburg Monarchy left an equally bitter legacy. The Austrian half of the Monarchy lost, in the north, the Czechs who joined their Slovak cousins from Hungary in a Czechoslovak Republic that contained, in the Sudetenland on its western frontier, a worrying minority of Germans. In the south they lost the Slovenes, who with their Croat cousins from Hungary linked their fortunes with the Serbs in a clumsily entitled 'Kingdom of the Serbs, Croats and Slovenes', later to be renamed Jugoslavia (south Slavia). They lost their Italian lands south of the Alps, including Trieste, their main port on the Adriatic; but the territories promised to Italy on the eastern shores of the Adriatic were now in the possession of the 'liberated' Jugoslavs, who themselves had claims on Trieste and its hinterland. The German-speaking rump that was all that remained of Austria initially tried to join the new German republic to the north, but this was forbidden by the Allies. So Austria remained independent for a further twenty years until 1938, when an *Anschluss* was achieved to universal popular acclaim by one of her former citizens, Adolf Hitler. The Hungarians lost not only the Slovaks to the north and the Croats to the south, but the province of Transylvania in the east to a greatly enlarged Rumania, suffering an ugly little civil war in the process. The right-wing dictator who emerged from the mêlée, Admiral Horthy, refused to admit that the abdication of the Habsburgs had been valid at all and declared that he ruled merely as regent on their behalf. He continued to do so until he was himself overthrown at the end of the Second World War.

## *Turkey*

As for the Turks, initially they were treated as harshly as the Germans. Not only did they lose their possessions in the Arabian peninsula to new states under French or British control—Syria, Lebanon, Iraq, Saudi Arabia, Palestine, Transjordan—but they were invaded by Italian forces staking claims to Adalia under the Treaty of London of 1915, and by Greeks staking claims in Thrace and regions in Anatolia, especially Smyrna (Izmir), where there was a substantial Greek minority. Popular resentment at this diktat brought to power a new regime under Mustapha Kemal Ataturk, which drove the Greeks out of Anatolia and threatened to do the same to British forces occupying the Straits. After three confused years a settlement was reached at Lausanne in 1923, leaving Turkey in sole control of Anatolia and the Straits—with guarantees for their demilitarization—together with a foothold on Europe in eastern Thrace. The Greek population of Smyrna was brutally expelled, and disputes between Greece and Turkey over possession of islands in the Aegean continued until, and beyond, the end of the century.

The peace settlement at Versailles has had a bad press, but most of its provisions have stood the test of time. The new states it created survived, if within fluctuating frontiers, until the last decade of the century, when the Czechs and Slovaks peacefully separated and Jugoslavia, always volatile, disintegrated and threatened new wars in the process. The Franco-German frontier was stabilized. 'The Eastern Question' arising from Turkey's presence in Europe was solved for good. But 'the German Question' remained unsolved. In spite of her defeat, Germany remained the most powerful nation in Europe, and determined to reverse the settlement at least of her eastern frontiers. France's attempt to restore a balance was doomed by ideological mistrust of the Soviet Union, by the weakness of her allies in East Europe, and by the profound reluctance of her people ever to endure a comparable ordeal again. The British were equally reluctant: their domestic and imperial problems, combined with the dreadful image of war that increasingly haunted the popular imagination, led successive governments to seek a solution in appeasing German demands rather than resisting them. As for the United States, their intervention in Europe was widely seen as having been a bad mistake, and one never to be repeated.

When the terms of the treaty were announced, a prescient American cartoonist depicted Wilson, Lloyd George, and Clemenceau emerging from the Paris peace conference, one saying 'Curious: I seem to hear a child weeping.' And sure enough, hiding behind a pillar, there was a little boy crying his heart out, with the words '1940 Class' inscribed over his head.

# Appendix I. President Wilson's Fourteen Points

Wilson laid down his 'Fourteen Points' in a message to Congress on 8 January 1918. They were as follows:

I. Open covenants of peace, openly arrived at . . .

II. Absolute freedom of navigation upon the seas, outside territorial waters, alike in peace and in war . . .

III. The removal, so far as possible, of all economic barriers and the establishment of an equality of trade conditions among all the nations consenting to the peace . . .

IV. . . . [N]ational armaments to be reduced to the lowest point consistent with public safety.

V. . . . [I]mpartial adjustment of all colonial claims.

VI. The evacuation of all Russian territory . . .

VII. Belgium . . . must be evacuated and restored, without any attempt to delimit the sovereignty which she enjoys in common with all free nations.

VIII. All French territory should be freed and the invaded provinces restored, and the wrong done to France by Prussia in 1871 in the matter of Alsace-Lorraine . . . should be righted . . .

IX. A readjustment of the frontiers of Italy should be effected along clearly recognizable lines of nationality.

X. The peoples of Austria-Hungary . . . should be accorded the freest opportunity for autonomous development.

XI. Rumania, Serbia and Montenegro should be evacuated; occupied territories restored; Serbia accorded free and secure access to the sea . . .

XII. The Turkish portions of the present Ottoman Empire should be assured a secure sovereignty, but the other nationalities which are now under Turkish rule should be assured an undoubted security of life and absolutely unmolested opportunity of autonomous development . . .

XIII. An independent Polish state should be erected which should include the territories inhabited by indisputably Polish populations, which should be assured a free and secure access to the sea . . .

XIV. A general association of nations must be formed under specific covenants for the purpose of affording mutual guarantees of political independence and territorial integrity to great and small states alike.

# Appendix II. Total War Casualties

|  | Population | Mobilized | Dead |
|---|---|---|---|
| *Central Powers* | | | |
| Austria-Hungary | 52m. | 7.8m. | 1,200,000 |
| Germany | 67m. | 11.0m. | 1,800,000 |
| Turkey | | 2.8m. | 320,000 |
| Bulgaria | | 1.2m. | 90,000 |
| *Allies* | | | |
| France | 36.5m. | 8.4m. | 1,400,000 |
| Britain | 46m. | 6.2m. | 740,000 |
| British Empire | | 2.7m. | 170,000 |
| Russia | 164m. | 12.0m. | 1,700,000 |
| Italy | 37m. | 5.6m. | 460,000 |
| USA | 93m. | 4.3m. | 115,000 |

# Further Reading

Since the bibliography of the First World War is so immense, it is best for the beginner to start with a few general studies and go on from there.

The best survey of the war's origins, summarizing all the relevant controversies, is James Joll, *The Origins of the First World War* (London 1984). The war itself in all its aspects is well covered in Hew Strachan (ed.), *The Oxford Illustrated History of the First World War* (Oxford 1998). Of Strachan's own magisterial study only the first of three volumes has so far been published, *The First World War, i. To Arms* (Oxford 2000). This takes events in Europe only to the end of 1914, but deals so effectively with broader aspects of the conflict as to be already indispensable. Martin Gilbert, *The First World War* (London 1994) provides a useful chronicle, heavily illustrated with anecdote and pictures.

Most works by British historians, including this one, inevitably have something of an anglocentric bias and focus perhaps unduly on the Western Front. This needs to be corrected by reading Norman Stone, *The Eastern Front* (London 1975) and Holger H. Herwig, *The First World War: Germany and Austria-Hungary* (London 1997). On specifically national contributions read J. M. Bourne, *Britain and the Great War* (London 1989); J. F. Becker, *The Great War and the French People* (Leamington Spa 1985); Roger Chickering, *Imperial Germany and the Great War* (Cambridge 1998); and David Kennedy, *Over Here; the Great War and American Society* (New York 1980).

On economic aspects of the war Gerd Hardach, *The First World War 1914–1918* (London 1977) is succinct but comprehensive. Niall Ferguson, *The Pity of War* (London 1998) contains much important information in an otherwise controversial text.

# Index

The European powers were ready for war in 1914. Germany, fuelled by 'archaic militarism, global ambitions, and neurotic insecurity', took the offensive, in the misguided belief that it would shorten the conflict. Four years later, eight million people had died in the most apocalyptic episode the world had known.

Sir Michael Howard, pre-eminent military historian and author of such definitive works as *The Franco-Prussian War* and *War in European History*, has meditated on the subject of the First World War for several decades. The result is a 'masterpiece of concision' (Hew Strachan), a succinct and highly readable account of the events leading up to, and culminating in that conflict. With tremendous precision and clarity of vision he describes the effects of the conflict on soldiers and civilians alike, examining the military manoeuvres of the Allies and the rival alliances: the inhumane deployment of poison gas on the battlefield, the accelerated development of mechanized warfare, the establishment of the Royal Air Force in Britain, and the war at sea, which would draw America into the conflict. He highlights how the war fought at home – against the shortages of food, fuel, and raw materials for industry – caused the irreversible decline in German morale, a demise which was to lead to the eventual surrender of the German state.

Humiliated and bankrupt, utterly disempowered, Germany would never lose the belief that the war had been imposed upon her by the Allies. It would be that sense of injustice that would resonate through the decades to follow – to find final, chilling retribution in the hands of the Third Reich.